Cambridge Elements

Elements in Reinventing Capitalism
edited by
Arie Y. Lewin
Duke University
Till Talaulicar
University of Erfurt

STATE PLATFORM CAPITALISM

The United States, China, and the Global Battle for Digital Supremacy

Steve Rolf
University of Sussex

Seth Schindler
University of Manchester

Shaftesbury Road, Cambridge CB2 8EA, United Kingdom

One Liberty Plaza, 20th Floor, New York, NY 10006, USA

477 Williamstown Road, Port Melbourne, VIC 3207, Australia

314–321, 3rd Floor, Plot 3, Splendor Forum, Jasola District Centre,
New Delhi – 110025, India

Cambridge University Press is part of Cambridge University Press & Assessment, a department of the University of Cambridge.

We share the University's mission to contribute to society through the pursuit of education, learning and research at the highest international levels of excellence.

www.cambridge.org
Information on this title: www.cambridge.org/9781009619714

DOI: 10.1017/9781009446594

© Steve Rolf and Seth Schindler 2025

This publication is in copyright. Subject to statutory exception and to the provisions of relevant collective licensing agreements, with the exception of the Creative Commons version the link for which is provided below, no reproduction of any part may take place without the written permission of Cambridge University Press & Assessment.

An online version of this work is published at doi.org/10.1017/9781009446594 under a Creative Commons Open Access license CC-BY-NC 4.0 which permits re-use, distribution and reproduction in any medium for non-commercial purposes providing appropriate credit to the original work is given and any changes made are indicated. To view a copy of this license visit https://creativecommons.org/licenses/by-nc/4.0

When citing this work, please include a reference to the DOI 10.1017/9781009446594

First published 2025

A catalogue record for this publication is available from the British Library

ISBN 978-1-009-61971-4 Hardback
ISBN 978-1-009-44658-7 Paperback
ISSN 2634-8950 (online)
ISSN 2634-8942 (print)

Cambridge University Press & Assessment has no responsibility for the persistence or accuracy of URLs for external or third-party internet websites referred to in this publication and does not guarantee that any content on such websites is, or will remain, accurate or appropriate.

For EU product safety concerns, contact us at Calle de José Abascal, 56, 1°, 28003 Madrid, Spain, or email eugpsr@cambridge.org

State Platform Capitalism

The United States, China, and the Global Battle for Digital Supremacy

Elements in Reinventing Capitalism

DOI: 10.1017/9781009446594
First published online: November 2025

Steve Rolf
University of Sussex

Seth Schindler
University of Manchester

Author for correspondence: Steve Rolf, steverolf@gmail.com

Abstract: Global capitalism is being reshaped by two major trends. States have become increasingly interventionist, reshaping their economies in response to crises and geopolitical tensions. Secondly, digital platform giants have emerged from the United States and China that concentrate political economic power in private hands. This Element argues that these trends are increasingly symbiotic. Digital platforms are being folded into the spiralling rivalry between the United States and China. As states tap into their extraterritorial governance capacities by exerting control over platforms, platform firms leverage state support to pursue and expand their internationalization strategies. Therefore, the US–China rivalry is increasingly being fought at the level of the technology stack, a dynamic the authors call state platform capitalism. The Element examines four fields in which this novel regime of competition is at play: digital currencies, technical standards, cybersecurity, and smart cities. This Element is also available as Open Access on Cambridge Core.

Keywords: Political Economy, State capitalism, Digital platforms, digital business models, geopolitical conflict

© Steve Rolf and Seth Schindler 2025

ISBNs: 9781009619714 (HB), 9781009446587 (PB), 9781009446594 (OC)
ISSNs: 2634-8950 (online), 2634-8942 (print)

Contents

1 Introduction	1
Part I A New Paradigm	**8**
2 State Platform Capitalism: Theory and History	8
3 The US Stack	21
4 The Chinese Stack	30
Part II Spheres of Competition	**42**
5 Digital Currencies	43
6 Cybersecurity	48
7 Standards	54
8 Smart Cities	59
9 Conclusion	64
References	66

# 1 Introduction

1.1 Calling All Influencers

Visitors to the US Capitol building in Washington, DC, on March 22, 2023, were greeted by a curious scene. A group of demonstrators chanted slogans, bore placards, and spoke to a group of reporters gathered at the scene. But their immaculate hairstyles, expensive watches, and luxury sunglasses betrayed that these were not campaigners against war or racial injustice. They were social media influencers, and their demand was to 'Keep TikTok'. They hoped to influence congressional representatives as they debated the fate of the short video app.

Inside Congress, lawmakers grilled TikTok's US CEO, Shou Zi Chew, on the company's handling of US citizens' data, the nature of its relationship with its Chinese parent company ByteDance, and its purported links to the Chinese Communist Party (CCP). The demonstrators outside were unable to influence the mood on Capitol Hill. Evidently unsatisfied with Mr. Chew's answers, in March 2024, the Senate passed a bill forcing ByteDance to sell its stake in TikTok or face a ban on operating in the United States. The 'TikTok Bill' (Protecting Americans from Foreign Adversary Controlled Applications Act, PAFACA) will help ensure that the US digital media ecosystem remains under firm control of domestic firms like Meta (Facebook), X (formerly Twitter), and Google.[1]

These events are illuminating for three reasons. First, they highlight how growing concerns about the social power of digital media platforms – including their data collection and sharing practices, and the impacts of their algorithms on public life – are increasingly driving oversight and policymaking efforts. Second, they represent the US government's political response to TikTok, which is the first major Chinese digital platform to succeed in the US market (since followed by retail platform apps such as Shein and Temu). The case suggests the United States is willing to use the full spectrum of its policy toolkit to inhibit Chinese platforms from gaining market share in the United States, and to protect the dominance of its digital platform firms against Chinese competitors. Third, they demonstrate that platforms have become increasingly central to the broader US-China geopolitical rivalry, a competition which is increasingly reshaping world politics and the economy.

How did apparently innocuous internet platform companies like TikTok, Meta, and Google – known principally for their banal functionalities like

---

[1] At the time of writing, President Trump appears to have secured a deal, where ByteDance will sell TikTok to a consortium of investors apparently led by Oracle's Larry Ellison. Bytedance will retain a minority stake in the new firm, to which it will license its algorithm. Oracle will store user data within the US and control how the TikTok algorithm operates.

short video content and search optimization algorithms – become entangled with the logic of a global geopolitical conflict? As we show in the following pages, platforms increasingly provide the infrastructure undergirding the world's social and economic networks. Not only do they facilitate and intermediate the countless exchanges that comprise much of daily life, but they increasingly hold the power to (re)shape how, and even to decide if, these interactions take place. This *infrastructural* role affords them tremendous power, because they write the rules – both metaphorically and literally, in devising their 'terms of service' – by which other social and economic agents interact. If 'code is law', as Lawrence Lessig (2000) once wrote, then platforms represent planetary-scale judiciaries. What is more, platforms' infrastructural power – manifest in their vast capital, compute, and data resources – is placing them at the centre of the global race to develop and commercialize artificial intelligence (AI) (Nitzberg and Zysman, 2022; van der Vlist et al., 2024).

This steady accumulation of power by platform firms has not gone unnoticed in the corridors of political power. But, as we aim to demonstrate, the response to growing platform power from politicians has not been entirely hostile. In addition to curtailing some of the powers their domestic platform firms wield at home, governments in Washington, Beijing, and elsewhere have concurrently sought to bolster the global standing of their largest platform firms abroad. In this way, states are beginning to recognize the large potential for multiplying their power which can derive from harnessing platform infrastructure for public ends. And although platform firms are often hostile to new regulatory initiatives and regimes, they have increasingly partnered with states because of the economic and regulatory advantages that this affords.

1.2 Conflict and State Capitalism

Digital platforms did not arise in a vacuum. Their rise to become global economic powerhouses was propelled by the rules and institutions that underpinned neoliberal globalization in the 1990s and 2000s. The basic principle of US power after the Cold War was to open the world's markets ever more deeply to free flows of investment, trade, and information. With the 'Washington Consensus', US policymakers pushed states towards ever-greater marketization, dismantling the edifice of post-war statism, and empowering global institutions such as the WTO to invigilate these new rules. The United States privatized the networking infrastructure which had emerged through its efforts to interconnect local networks under the auspices of D/ARPA, while encouraging (through consent and coercion) third countries to follow suit (Tarnoff, 2022). The new US internet firms which emerged consolidated market power by amalgamating the hitherto local networks built up within the United States into a national 'internet'. But they also spread rapidly across borders and markets, protected by a global IP regime and encouraged by the liberal prescriptions for the world to pursue development and growth through networked integration (embodied by the WTO's 1997 Basic Telecommunications Agreement).

Neoliberal globalization was underpinned by optimistic narrative of liberal peace underpinned by economic integration. In this 'flat' world, developing countries would supposedly be unencumbered by the demands of great powers or threatening neighbours. In exchange for opening their markets to firms from the developed countries, they could leverage their distinctive advantages to achieve growth and prosperity. Transnational economic integration instantiated a 'partial shift of some components of state sovereignty to other institutions' such as multinational corporations and international organizations (Sassen, 1996, 146).

However, neoliberalism did not simply erode state power (Comunello and Mulargia, 2023). Rather, some states and some firms gained considerable influence and control over the strategic flows and nodes that underpinned global networks, even as others saw their power wane. So even while economies became increasingly interdependent through radical increases in flows of goods, trade, and investment, power relations remained profoundly asymmetric. Critically, the United States was able to maintain its handle on many (if not all) of the key 'chokepoints' within transnational networks.

Much of this new architecture of networked power remained hidden from view until conflicts over networks burst into the open during the first Trump presidency (Farrell and Newman, 2023). Trump's first administration made clear that great power competition had not been superseded by globalization. Since he launched his 'trade war' on China early during his first term, the United States and China have become locked in an increasingly intense and all-encompassing rivalry increasingly analogous to the Cold War (Schindler et al., 2024). But in contrast to the Cold War, which produced a world divided economically into largely isolated territorial blocs, contemporary geopolitical rivalry is unfolding in the networked world that globalization built (Schindler and Rolf, 2024). Rather than a great unravelling of globalized networks, events since 2016 have driven states to radically expand their definitions of national security to include the ability to secure supply chains, access internationally integrated financial systems, and develop new technologies in innovation networks (Drezner, 2024). This expansive definition of national security – while it has encouraged states to make ever-deeper interventions to securitize their economies – has not yet undermined globalization in aggregate (Babić et al., 2022).

The state capitalist tools to which states have turned in pursuit of security and/ or geoeconomic leverage have deeper roots in the decades-long downward trend in global economic growth. The aforementioned neoliberal market reforms which drove globalization were supposed to allocate resources more efficiently and revive economic dynamism, but the results were underwhelming. The 2008 global financial prompted dramatic and long-lasting fiscal and monetary interventions to stabilize their economies and maintain liquidity. The quantitative easing undertaken by the US Treasury, combined with China's stimulus spending, came to represent more of a new paradigm than stopgap measures. State-owned enterprises have experienced a comeback as states sought to pursue strategic investment programmes (IMF, 2020), and well-endowed sovereign wealth funds have purchased large stakes in leading private firms. Large-scale infrastructure investment also made a revival (Schindler and Kanai, 2021), in part as a way of mopping up surplus capital, while the complex central bank financial engineering required to prop up stock markets in 2008 never went away – resulting in perennial asset price inflation (Adkins et al., 2020). The economic and financial crises driven by the COVID-19 pandemic simply deepened these interventionist trends in both countries and beyond (van Apeldoorn and de Graaff, 2022).

Taken together these trends have been labelled as a 'new' form of state capitalism (Musacchio et al., 2015; Alami and Dixon, 2020b), most notable for the way in which it goes far beyond simple state-ownership to encompass a variety of novel interventionist strategies. And state capitalism has become wrapped up with geopolitical competition, as states vie to secure their economies against rivals through ever greater and deeper interventions (Alami et al., 2025). The emergent result is the rise of an increasingly multipolar world order, both increasingly geopolitically-fragmented while nevertheless marked by 'deep' forms of international economic integration both inside and between blocs (Lewin, 2024; Mezzadra and Neilson, 2024; Wijaya and Jayasuriya, 2024). State capitalist practices and their geopolitical corollaries have begun to remake the platform economy in dramatic new ways.

1.3 Platforms in the Ascendancy

State capitalism wasn't the only major development to grow out of the 2008 global financial crisis. In the years of stagnation which followed, investment capital flooded en masse into the US tech sector. This fuelled an unprecedented investment boom, as start-ups sought to 'hyperscale' their way to market dominance by leveraging freely flowing venture capital (Klinge et al., 2023; Varoufakis, 2024).

Big tech and the proliferating platform business model represented the best venue for capital seeking out returns in a broader environment of stagnation (Rikap and Lundvall, 2021). Rather than competing in oversaturated markets for particular product lines, platforms compete with one another to intermediate social and economic exchanges between users at scale (Srnicek, 2017). For platform firms, securing first-mover advantage is a matter of survival because they operate in 'winner-take-most' markets (Brynjolfsson and McAfee (2014). Success often means establishing a 'digital ecosystem' that serves as a 'market maker' insofar as users are locked in, network effects take hold, and rival platforms struggle to attract users or complementors (Gawer, 2022). After the 2008 crisis, the abundance of cheap capital combined with rock-bottom interest rates allowed platform firms to expand at breakneck speed. Profits became virtually passé as platforms focused on 'growth at all costs' – and often at exorbitant cost to investors. Capital was ploughed into (making or buying) innovations in software, but also very tangible assets such as data centres and network infrastructure. While they were slow to come, the gains being chased were real for those platforms that could establish a dominant position. After years of losses, Silicon Valley giants like Facebook, Google, and Amazon generated $90 bn in profits in the pandemic year of 2020 (Tarnoff, 2022).

As platform firms have proliferated, they have come to intermediate an ever greater quantity of routine social and economic interactions. The burgeoning 'platformization' of everyday life means ordering food, hailing a cab, messaging a friend, or paying for goods is increasingly difficult – if not impossible – without the exchange being intermediated by one (or many) US technology firms. It is not just consumers who cannot avoid the platform giants. Global businesses and governments too have come to depend upon the data centres, software, networking equipment, and financial technologies owned and operated by platform giants to conduct their everyday business. Platforms have consequently become the critical infrastructure upon which other sectors of the economy and society rely for their everyday functioning. The newfound powers of such 'private infrastructure' providers have led to growing concern for state sovereignty and capacity (Rahman, 2018). Some have argued that their power has grown so large that they have suspended the rule of capitalism altogether (Varoufakis, 2024).

But despite what seems to be their growing global dominance, US tech giants do face mounting competition. The threat of regulation by foreign governments – so far held largely at bay by Washington – looms large (Bradford, 2023). But more strikingly, they confront mounting commercial competition from the country which contains their only serious rivals: China. Beijing inhibited the operations of Silicon Valley tech giants in China throughout the

2000s. As they amassed nearly unassailable market positions in many countries, they largely struggled to gain a foothold in China. This left space for domestic Chinese firms to grow and innovate. Although still considerably smaller in scale and value, today, China's platform giants are increasingly venturing overseas and competing directly with their US rivals. In some market sectors Chinese platforms like Huawei, Tiktok, Shein, Alibaba, and ZTE can win. Huawei has no US rival in the field of 5/6 G networking and is mounting a real challenge to US opponents in the chip and AI sector, while Chinese media platform TikTok is stealing a march on American rivals across large parts of the world. Alibaba and Tencent are increasingly important players in cloud computing, while these and other firms offer a growing range of vital services to global markets such as e-government technologies, smart cities, health tech, and AI.

US institutions have voiced mounting alarm at the rapid growth of Chinese platform firms. For instance, China's Belt and Road Initiative has facilitated the expansion of China's global port investments. Chinese-owned ports typically deploy a logistics management platform called LOGINK that intermediates relations among shippers, receivers, port operators, and regulators. By integrating and sharing shipping data amongst these users, LOGINK provides essential functions that underpin global trade. It also writes the rules by which its users interact, which affords it significant power in trade and production networks. The US government interprets integration of this digital software with port infrastructure as a threat because 'China's government may use insights gleaned from LOGINK to expand and more precisely target its use of economic coercion. Data aggregated through the platform may enable China to block or disrupt trade flows' to its enemies' (USCC Staff, 2022). Importantly, the US government does not allege that China has actually *done* any of these things, but it fears widespread use of the LOGINK platform gives Beijing a strategic network position that has the *potential* to be weaponized.

1.4 An Emergent Global Regime of Competition

As the LOGINK example indicates, platforms do far more than intermediate relations among buyers and sellers. They also regulate and govern interactions between third parties, and extract an extraordinary amount of valuable data in the process. This expansive power to govern through code has led many commentators to understand large platform firms as alternative power centres to nation-states. According to some, firms like Google are simply too expansive and complex for states to regulate, while their rules and investment strategies continue to disrupt and reshape growing swathes of the real economy (Gu, 2023).

This points to an apparent tension between the emergence of a new state capitalism and the platformization of the global economy. On the one hand, states are reasserting their role as regulators and direct economic actors worldwide. But on the other hand, the world's largest private platform corporations exercise control over the digital infrastructure upon which states' power – and society at large – increasingly depends. By intermediating and governing relations, platforms 'enclose markets' within their boundaries in ways which appears to pose a threat to states' political prerogative (Staab, 2024). How might we reconcile this purported rise of a new state capitalism with the simultaneous and unprecedented rise in private corporate power?

Our core contention is that far from representing a contradiction, a confluence of interest between states and platforms has emerged. In the context of growing geopolitical hostilities, the United States and China increasingly instrumentalize platforms because their ability to enclose markets and exert regulatory power afford novel opportunities to exercise power. Meanwhile, platform firms' ambition to expand their digital ecosystems and internationalize operations has become dependent upon states. Governments act as patrons that shield platform firms from regulatory measures in foreign jurisdictions, provide direct subsidies and other preferential forms of treatment, and are the source of lucrative contracts which fund innovation and investment. This is not to deny the tensions, sometimes significant, between digital platform firms and their home states. Nevertheless, we contend that these conflicts are closer to footnotes than headlines in the story we present – states increasingly attempt to secure the global power of 'their' digital platforms as a means to exercizing extraterritorial forms of power, while platform firms welcome sustained support from states to bolster and secure their international operations.

This symbiotic relationship between states and platform firms, in the context of growing geopolitical rivalry, animates the emergence of a new kind of global political economic competition. We introduce the concept of *state platform capitalism* (SPC) to identify and theorize this novel and emergent regime of competition: in which platform firms and states cooperate in their mutual attempts to achieve control over – and weaponize if necessary – the hardware and software that underpin exchanges within the global economy (Rolf and Schindler, 2023).

Clearly, not all states are equal in this global rivalry. Indeed, the two global centres of state platform capitalism today are the United States and China. This Element is about how their drive to platformize the world's data flows has spilled over into a structure of global competition, with states and platform firms playing distinct but complementary roles in this contest for supremacy. Platform competition looks quite different from traditional capitalist competition – it encompasses conflicts *between ecosystems* rather than conflicts *for market share in particular product lines* (Cennamo, 2021). Thus, state platform capitalist competition is fought out in ways and in spheres quite different from older forms of market or geopolitical competition. Our purpose here is to identify how SPC competition operates, and with what consequences.

This text is divided into two sections. The first section conceptualizes state platform capitalism and charts its rise. After presenting a historically informed theoretical framework in Section 1, Sections 2 and 3 examine, respectively, the US and Chinese varieties of SPC. We explain how these national varieties of SPC emerged, identify their key actors, and describe their organizational features and dynamics. We demonstrate how in both cases varied forms of state-firm interaction are increasingly oriented towards expanding the international reach of platforms, while simultaneously bolstering the geostrategic objectives of states. In this way, while acknowledging its distinct national manifestations, we emphasize the *systemic* character of SPC – and especially how its 'varieties' are conditioned by their interaction and competition. The second section explores how SPC animates distinctive forms of competition in a range of fields. Section 4 explores its implications for battles over digital currencies, while Section 5 reviews the competition to control future 'smart cities'. Section 6 narrates the competition to establish digital standards (both formal and de facto), and Section 7 focuses on cybersecurity. We conclude by reflecting on the implications of SPC for the future of digital connectivity and the global political economy more generally.

Part I A New Paradigm

2 State Platform Capitalism: Theory and History

2.1 Introduction

Amidst the global health emergency and socio-economic turmoil unleashed by the COVID-19 pandemic, observers could have been forgiven for missing a conspicuous datapoint. In 2020, the ratio of US government federal spending to GDP reached an all-time high, surpassing even that achieved at the height of mobilization for total war in 1944–5 (IMF, 2024). The interventions required to prop up economies during the pandemic lockdowns were not a complete aberration; however. government spending across advanced economies has been on a steady (though fluctuating) upward trajectory ever since the end of the Second World War. The 2008 financial crisis and the COVID-19 pandemic simply accelerated this trend. Along with the perpetually rising economic profile of states, *state capitalist* practices and policy interventions have both made a dramatic return and evolved in new ways. From the expansion of sovereign wealth funds and policy banks to proliferating industrial and technology policies, and full-blown economic nationalism, state interventions in the economy have proliferated on a global scale (Alami and Dixon, 2024).

The re-emergence of state capitalism has coincided with an epochal shift in the organization of capitalist firms: the rise of digital platform companies to the commanding heights of the global economy. Tech firms' boosters welcome a 'second machine age' of 'brilliant technologies' which promise dramatic increases in productivity and wealth (Brynjolfsson and McAfee, 2014). Meanwhile critics argue that big tech amounts to extractive, parasitic organizations driving economies towards 'techno-feudalism', in which predatory tech elites extract labour from digital serfs amidst economic stagnation (Durand, 2020; Varoufakis, 2024). Amidst this debate, there is broad consensus that digital platform firms have increasingly come to exercise 'state-like' governance functions that erode the power of public authorities (Lehdonvirta, 2022; Törnberg, 2023). As platforms continue to expand, governments are understood to be waging a zero-sum 'global battle to regulate technology' – one which they are commonly understood to be losing (Bradford, 2023).

State capitalism and platform capitalism, then, appear to represent deeply contradictory trends. On one hand, states' role as economic actors continues to multiply and intensify. Yet on the other hand, states seem powerless to regulate the largest platform firms such as Google, Amazon, and Alibaba. Which is it? And which side will win out? We present an alternative view. We show how contemporary state capitalist and platform capitalist practices – while initially distinctive and relatively autonomous trends – share deep historical roots, were both significantly driven by the global economic crises of 2008 and 2020, and are mutually reinforcing rather than contradictory trends.

Our starting point is to claim that state capitalism and platform capitalism should be conceived in the first instance as *organizational* and *institutional* 'fixes' to the structural problems encountered by global capitalism (Peck and Tickell, 1994; Alami and Dixon, 2020a). The concept of a *fix* was first developed by Harvey (1981) in order to identify how capitalists and state managers devise temporary solutions to the structural crisis tendencies that frequently disrupt capitalist accumulation. They may engineer moves of money from manufacturing into real estate and infrastructure or into underdeveloped regions or economies (spatial fix), restructure businesses, outsource and offshore activities (organizational fix), or restructure policy environments to secure new avenues for growth (institutional fix). However, rather than resolving crises, fixes tend to defer, displace or redirect them. As such, fixes forestall crises, but they create novel contradictions that ultimately culminate in new crises: such is the crisis-prone nature of capitalism.

This section first identifies how a rejuvenation of state capitalist practices was significantly driven by the dynamics of a global economic slowdown in 2008, before becoming imbricated with geopolitical competition. The urgency of rescuing banking sectors and industrial producers both forced states to break with (self-imposed) laissez-faire of the globalization years, but also revealed what had always been true: that capitalist economies are underpinned by state power. But state capitalist dynamics became increasingly (geo)politicized due to the *uneven and combined* dynamics at play in the global political economy (Alami and Dixon, 2021). As some states pursue these practices somewhat successfully, others are driven to imitate and adapt to keep up. In this way, policy instruments which emerged as crisis-management tools are becoming deployed for geopolitical ends, with the effect of legitimating their use and strengthening the aspirations of other states to exert control over their own economies.

Next, we turn to the rise of digital capitalism and the platform business model. Although digitalization has a long history, the rise of giant digital platforms to pre-eminence in the global economy is equally tied up with the crisis of 2008 (Srnicek, 2017). We map the evolution of platform business strategies within this broader political economy context. Finally, we demonstrate that rather than being fundamentally opposing trends, state capitalism and platform capitalism are complementary, and increasingly dovetail with one another. As governments embrace state capitalism in their attempts to bolster national security, it is only logical that they seek to exploit the tremendous governance capabilities and extraterritorial reach of platform firms. Platforms, meanwhile, seek to bolster their international scale and scope by obtaining state protection and patronage. The fusion of the distinct but convergent logics of state and platform capitalism is, we claim, fuelling a novel mode of competition between the United States and Chinese states and their platform firms, which we elaborate in the remainder of the text. As with all such 'fixes', however, dynamic contradictions and tensions are built-in to this mode of competition – and how these manifest is the major focus of the second part of the Element.

2.2 State Capitalism

State capitalism has a long history. The concept first was introduced with reference to concentrated industrial trusts which were increasingly tied up with the state, alongside emergent forms of national ownership, in late nineteenth-century Europe (Sperber, 2019). Since then, it has passed through many permutations, being used (variously) to signify diverse organizational systems: from the Soviet Union's centralized planning apparatus and the Keynesian policy frameworks of the advanced economies during the post-war period, to the 'illiberal', state-directed and resource-based economies of contemporary Russia, Iran, and Venezuela (Kurlantzick, 2016).

In this Element, we seek conceptual clarity by drawing on advances made by the literature on the 'new state capitalism' (Alami and Dixon, 2024). Much writing broadly conceived of the neoliberal period as a 'retreat of the state' from governing the economy (Konings, 2010). This conceptualization understood economies to existent on a spectrum between 'liberal' and 'coordinated' market economies – with commentators treating those not fitting the ideal types as state capitalist aberrations, limited to a handful of middle-income and developing economies like Russia, Turkey, and China (e.g., Bremmer, 2009). Such work ignored the considerable support (both financial and in terms of coordination) states offered to their firms right through the neoliberal period (Alami and Dixon, 2020b). It also offered a poor means by which to grasp how or why a dramatic expansion of highly visible and direct statist interventions have proliferated on a global scale – across virtually all varieties of capitalist economy.

By contrast, following Alami and Dixon (2024), we conceptualize state capitalism not as an ideal type or a variety of capitalism, but as a set of processes and relationships by which states seek to actively support the process of capital accumulation. Understood in this way, state capitalism is conceived as a perennial feature of real capitalist economies – but also that as a set of practices, it is potentially subject to transformation, evolution, and increases (or decreases) in scale and scope over time. There is indeed both continuity and innovation in contemporary state capitalist practices (Musacchio et al., 2015). They range from what Alami and Dixon (2021, 765) identify as 'state-capital hybrids' like sovereign wealth firms, state-owned (or backed) firms and policy banks; to the 'muscular statism' of industrial and innovation policies, capital controls, and development and planning strategies. And while many interventions are underpinned by economic nationalism, the new state capitalism is simultaneously transnational in character. Far from acting in ways which fragment the globalized economy, sovereign wealth funds (SWFs) and state-owned enterprises (SOEs) are major drivers of transnational economic integration as they pursue expansive overseas investments (Babić et al., 2022).

Understood in this way, it is clear that state capitalist practices have dramatically increased in both scale and scope over the past decade and a half. What drove the emergence of the new state capitalism? The global financial crisis of

2008 punctured deep-seated assumptions about the smooth evolution of neoliberal globalization. It generated far-reaching changes in the structures and dynamics of the world economy, most notably inaugurating a period of secular stagnation in growth and productivity. While these trends predate 2008 (Brenner, 2006), both were considerably worsened by the economic crisis and its aftermath. The economic turmoil initiated by lockdowns during the COVID-19 pandemic also simply served to accelerate these long-standing economic trends as states struggled to contain the economic fallout (van Apeldoorn and de Graaff, 2022). It was fundamentally the deepening of economic stagnation, punctuated by the economic crises of 2008 and 2020, which drove states to intervene in their economies in ever more intensive ways to support growth.

The effect of rising state capitalist interventions was often to stabilize or even boost growth for its practitioner economies. But at the same time, state capitalist practices have inevitably served to fragment the global economy. The IMF has warned of rising 'geoeconomic fragmentation' as states seek to exert control over their economies (Gopinath, 2024). International business scholars have identified how state capitalist practices have solidified the emergence of poles of political-economic power characterized by increasingly distinct regional market structures, supply opportunities, regulatory systems, and risk environments (Luo and Van Assche, 2023; Lewin, 2024; Luo and Tung, 2025). At the same time, states seek to exert greater control over global value chains which extend far beyond their national or regional territories, driving ongoing integration and tension between economic poles (Schindler and Rolf, 2024). These new state capitalist practices are the source of considerable geopolitical tensions, as they threaten to disrupt the relatively unified and open global economy which was forged during the neoliberal period (Alami et al., 2025). Indeed, statecraft is increasingly geared towards securing the conditions for long-term economic security and competitiveness, industrial and technological leadership, and resilience of critical supply chains and production networks (Weiss and Thurbon, 2020; Weiss, 2021). In this way, contemporary statist economic practices can be seen simultaneously as responses to and drivers of geopolitical tension.

Despite proliferating regional conflicts, the US-China rivalry represents the key geopolitical driver of this resurgence in state capitalist practices. Since the rapprochement between China and the United States during the later stages of the Cold War, US policy towards China remained largely consistent for three decades. Its principal focus was on pushing China to open its markets and financial sector to US and global investors, in exchange for receiving access to US markets and facilitating its entry into the global economy (especially via joining the WTO) (Rolf, 2021; Hung, 2022). Despite acceding to the WTO in

2001, China implemented neoliberal reforms only selectively, trimming but never dismantling its powerful state sector. At the same time, Beijing ramped up its spending on military capabilities in line with growth, as military spending became a key part of China's broader innovation ecosystem (Cheung, 2022). Pockets of support for pursuing more hardline neoliberal reform were fatally undermined by the global financial crisis of 2008, in the aftermath of which officials doubled down on 'state capitalist' practices. These included large-scale stimulus packages concentrating on infrastructure building, the launching of an expansive and expensive industrial policy in 2015 called *Made in China 2025* (Naughton and Tsai, 2015), and subsequently ploughing unprecedented quantities of funding towards strategic private sector fields like ICT and green technology (Naughton, 2020b).

The United States enacted a major foreign policy 'pivot to Asia' in 2011, explained at the time by US foreign policy elites as a response to China's mooted 'new assertiveness' (Shambaugh, 2020). In addition to re-asserting power in the Asia Pacific after a decade of war in the Middle East, this pivot was driven by a desire to prevent China from becoming a new centre of political-economic gravity in the global system (Turner and Parmar, 2020). Critically, the United States developed a Trans-Pacific Partnership (TPP) agreement, designed to freeze China out of regional trade and technology networks, though the agreement ultimately floundered during 2016 (Ravenhill, 2017).

The US pivot and TPP sat uneasily alongside the Obama administration's purported commitment to a 'liberal peace' power politics, and to ongoing engagement with China (Harris and Trubowitz, 2021). The Trump administration, by contrast, abandoned this long-standing 'Open Door' geopolitics (van Apeldoorn et al., 2023) in favour of a bluntly mercantilist trade policy. Initially, the objective was to reduce the US trade deficit with China by imposing a series of tariffs, but the mission quickly expanded to include targeting China's leading high-tech firms such as Huawei and ZTE. This profound and long-standing foreign policy shift was outlined in the 2017 US National Security Strategy. Not only did it identify China (alongside Russia) as the primary threat to national security (rather than non-state terrorist groups), but it rejected the notion that they could become partners through diplomatic engagement and economic integration:

> These competitions require the United States to rethink the policies of the past two decades – policies based on the assumption that engagement with rivals and their inclusion in international institutions and global commerce would turn them into benign actors and trustworthy partners. For the most part, this premise turned out to be false.

While Trump did reach a temporary trade accord with Xi Jinping's administration, the COVID-19 pandemic interrupted its implementation and relations collapsed. The Biden administration essentially embraced the Trumpian worldview, systematizing Trump's piecemeal initiatives into an increasingly comprehensive framework aimed at limiting China's integration with the global economic order, and maintaining US dominance in strategic high-technology sectors (Leoni, 2022). Trump's return in 2025 simply signalled the death knell for any hope of a reversion in US policy.

The scope for a reduction in geopolitical tension appears limited. Both the United States and China have deployed expansive state capitalist practices towards the rivalry, in ways which have permanently reconfigured the dynamics of their economies. China's party-state has deepened its reach across its economy, by expanding the influence of SOEs and in deepening control mechanisms over the private sector (Liu and Tsai, 2021; Pearson et al., 2021). Meanwhile, the United States has moved in a similar direction, albeit within ideological constraints imposed by its political system. Starrs and Germann (2021) observe sweeping changes in (1) the US tariff regime, designed to target Chinese imports in particular; (2) the inward investment regime, aimed at restricting Chinese firms' access to high-tech US companies; and (3) export regulations, which use technology export bans to target Chinese firms like ZTE and Huawei. Heightened local procurement requirements have also been enacted through the reformed implementation of the Buy American Act, alongside evidence for a growing consensus on the value of state-led investments in strategic technology development and mission-oriented development projects in areas such as supply-chain reshoring and 5 G provision (Baltz, 2022).

But despite recent ructions caused by the second Trump administration's imposition of tariffs, the costs of full economic decoupling between the US and China seem to remain prohibitive (Rosen and Gloudeman, 2021) – both for the economies themselves, and for third countries. The 'new state capitalism', far from autarchic, is instead substantially geared towards the establishment of control over the transnational networks that constitute the architecture of globalization (Schindler et al., 2023). China's Belt and Road Initiative (BRI), for instance, has extended China's reach across Eurasia, Africa, and Latin America through a sweeping range of state-backed infrastructural investment and development financing initiatives. The BRI has in turn prompted the entry of the US government directly into the infrastructure financing space with its Development Finance Corporation and the nascent US-led G7 'Partnership for Global Infrastructure and Investment' (PGII). So far, it these initiatives are much smaller than the BRI, and they have also failed to meet their modest objectives (Schindler

2.3 Platform Capitalism

> [W]hat is internet infrastructure? Of course, there are data centres and massive server farms. There are devices produced by a handful of companies, and operating systems ... we must also include labour and practice, content moderation, device manufacture in Shenzhen, rare earth mineral mining, etc. – all of which is infrastructure ... What affordances sit below the thing we are seeing on the surface? Who owns those affordances? These are the questions we should be answering. (Meredith Whittaker et al. 2020)

As state capitalist practices expanded during the 2010s, observers fixated on another, perhaps more dazzling, trend: the emergence of *platform capitalism*. More than simply the digitalization of economies and societies, platform capitalism is characterized by the astonishing ascendance of platform companies to the heights of the global economy (Table 1). Observers of *Forbes' Global 500* ranking of top corporations in 2007 would not find a technology company near its top-25 positions, which were dominated by oil producers, auto firms, and banks. But digital behemoths like Amazon, Google/Alphabet, and Apple skyrocketed to the top of such lists in the decade after 2008. As of 2025, seven of the world's twenty-five top firms by market value are platform businesses (Microsoft, Apple, Amazon, Alphabet, Meta, Tencent, and SAP; see Table 1). Other major hardware firms generate the bulk of their businesses by selling hardware and services to these digital giants (NVIDIA, TSMC, Broadcom, and ASML). And manufacturers of digital devices such as Samsung and Tesla employ platform business models, as does the retailer Walmart in its online marketplace.

Platforms, many of which predate the global economic crisis, grew rapidly in the post-crisis era. This is in large part because they offer a business strategy suited to a world of slow growth and low interest rates (Srnicek, 2017; Davis, 2022). Platforms' business strategies can in this way be understood as an 'organizational fix' to the challenge posed by secular stagnation of economies. In the 2010s, Western financial sectors were flush with cash thanks to quantitative easing, bond purchasing programmes, and other mechanisms put in place to prop up the financial sector. Of the estimated $35 trillion in credit created by central banks between 2009 and 2022, Varoufakis (2024) estimates that a large majority of the share invested in productive assets found its way into the platform economy. This took place via myriad mechanisms, including saturated corporate bond markets, which themselves generated soaring stock markets as

Table 1 Top-25 global firms by market capitalization, as of May 2025

Company	Market cap (USD)	Country	Industry
Microsoft	3.415 tn	USA	Technology
NVIDIA	3.334 tn	USA	Technology
Apple	2.973 tn	USA	Technology
Amazon	2.173 tn	USA	Retail/Technology
Alphabet (Google)	2.079 tn	USA	Technology
Meta Platforms (Facebook)	1.619 tn	USA	Technology
Saudi Aramco	1.611 tn	S. Arabia	Energy
Tesla	1.151 tn	USA	Automotive/Technology
Broadcom	1.129 tn	USA	Technology
Berkshire Hathaway	1.088 tn	USA	Conglomerate/Finance
TSMC	1.005 tn	Taiwan	Technology
Walmart	785.44 bn	USA	Retail
JPMorgan Chase	733.88 bn	USA	Finance
Visa	698.52 bn	USA	Finance
Eli Lilly	656.27 bn	USA	Pharmaceuticals
Tencent	579.54 bn	China	Technology
MasterCard	526.13 bn	USA	Finance
Netflix	507.78 bn	USA	Entertainment/Technology
Costco	462.22 bn	USA	Retail
Oracle	456.73 bn	USA	Technology
Exxon Mobil	440.31 bn	USA	Energy
Procter & Gamble	397.04 bn	USA	Consumer Goods
Johnson & Johnson	371.85 bn	USA	Pharmaceuticals
Home Depot	366.93 bn	USA	Retail
SAP	353.20 bn	Germany	Technology

Source: *Authors, using data from* https://companiesmarketcap.com/

investors became prepared to pay a premium for tech equity; a generalized inflation in asset prices; and a flood of private equity and venture capital into technology startups (which could be acquired, or have their innovations acquired, by hyperscalers) (Kenney and Zysman, 2019; Rikap, 2024).

Rather than deploying this capital towards traditional competition in (saturated) global markets by offering specific goods and services, platform firms instead aim to build business ecosystems in which their infrastructure intermediates exchanges between external users, developers, and (sometimes) advertisers (Kenney and Zysman, 2016). This requires typically very considerable investments in both tangibles and intangibles, R&D, and outlays on user recruitment (Klinge et al., 2023). Because platforms' services are substantially intangible, their low marginal cost affords opportunities to achieve *scale* and *scope* economies at breakneck speed, supported by the use of cloud computing (Narayan, 2022). Once critical scale has been achieved, the switching costs imposed by network effects serve as a powerful way of locking-in user bases. Margins on transactions are often tiny, but low margins can be offset with extremely high volume. And platforms operate across multiple horizontal business lines, using cross-subsidization to build attractive multi-service ecosystems (Thomas et al., 2024). Given their privileged access to financial markets, profitability is often less of an imperative (at least in the short term) for platform firms than their ability to scale. According to one estimate, platform firms will soon come to mediate one-third of all global economic activity (Dietz et al., 2020).

Broadly speaking, the open architecture of a platform constitutes a core-periphery model, in which core technologies are under the direct control of the platform firm, while third-party designers generate complementary innovations (Rodon Modol and Eaton, 2021). External developers' (complementors) innovations further enhance network and lock-in effects. The Apple Store, for instance, relies on third-party companies to build the majority of iOS apps which make the iPhone a useful and attractive device. But because platform firms maintain ownership of and control over their cores, they retain the authority and capacity to rewrite the rules (*protocols*) through which ecosystem users interact (Galloway, 2004). A core goal of platform protocol is to prevent so-called 'multihoming' and deepen user lock-in via technical means. Consequently, in certain sectors platform firms have become unavoidable intermediaries, mediating the exchange of goods and services amongst users within enclosed digital spaces (Langley and Leyshon, 2017).

As a function of being unavoidable intermediaries in transactions and exchanges, platform firms are able to leverage control over protocol to influence everyday habits and practices (Grön et al., 2023). Locking users into ecosystems enables platforms to extract payment from value circulating across platform networks (Sadowski, 2020; Arboleda and Purcell, 2021), but also to write the rules by which they interact. Staab (2024) consequently argues platforms represent the rise of *privatized marketplaces*. Innovations like algorithmically generated prices and supplier rankings systems disrupt market pricing mechanisms to the extent that the integrity of public markets – the cornerstone of capitalist economies – is potentially threatened. Furthermore, platforms' control over protocol also affords them enormous power to reshape the business processes of firms which use their infrastructure (Nowak et al., 2022). Consider, for instance, the ability of Apple to exert control over third-party apps in its App Store via terms of service.

Platform power is predicated upon the capability to integrate technology 'stacks': assemblages of global-scale computational hardware and software. Digital platforms constitute a user-friendly interface for efficiently navigating this subterranean 'infrastructural complex of server farms, massive databases, energy sources, optical cables, wireless transmission media, and distributed applications' (Bratton, 2016, 70). While this assemblage of devices and software is intrinsically open ('the open web'), platforms seek to wall off access to sections of these stacks using technical barriers, IP law, restricted access to APIs, and algorithmic filtering and curation. They monopolize the 'walled gardens' they create in a way that was impossible with the open internet (Plantin and De Seta, 2019; Peck and Phillips, 2021). In this way, platform competition is distinct from typical competition in lines for specific products or services. For Jacobides (2019), 'in a growing number of sectors, the firm and even the industry have ceased to be meaningful units of strategic analysis. We must focus instead on competition between digitally-enabled designed ecosystems that span traditional industry boundaries and offer complex and customisable product-service bundles'.

Like earlier vertically integrated corporations, platforms aim to minimize transaction costs and exercise market dominance. Yet, they differ markedly in some ways. Rather than employing vertical integrated command structures (Chandler Jr, 1977), they instead operate by organizing market interactions digitally, and exerting control through ecosystem governance via 'terms of service' commands rather than managerial hierarchies. The power to orchestrate and govern without owning represents a powerful evolution of corporate control strategies (Grabher, 2025).

The extreme corporate concentration and financial dominance of giant platform firms is represented by a distinctive economic geography with two main poles (Kenney and Zysman, 2020). The United States dominates, with the combined value of the so-called 'magnificent seven' technology firms (Alphabet, Amazon, Apple, Meta, Microsoft, NVIDIA, Tesla) representing about a third of US stock market value as of May 2025. China represents another pole of digital power in the global political economy (Figure 1). The platforms domiciled in both these countries have immense extraterritorial power, given they exercise considerable control over most of the world's technology stacks (Mayer and Lu, 2025)

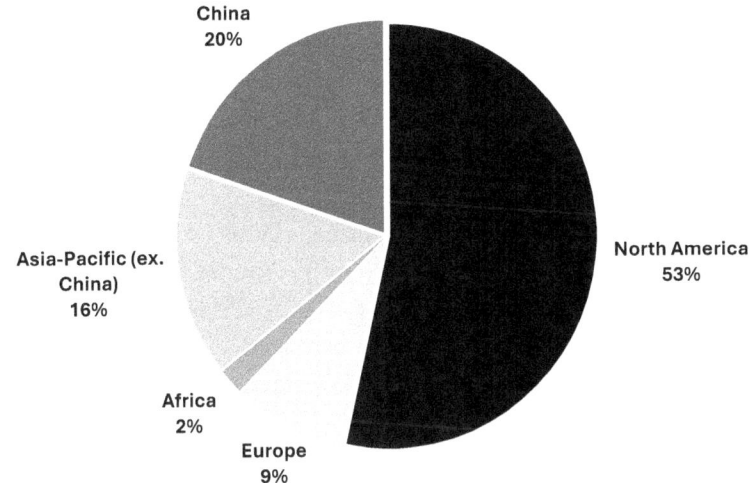

Figure 1 Top 101 global platform firms by region/country of domicile, 2023.
Source: *Data from Hosseini (2023) and authors.*

2.4 State Platform Capitalism

Rather than cutting against one another, the distinct logics of state and platform capitalism have coalesced in unanticipated and generative ways. The specific political-economic *affordances* that characterize the platform business model are increasingly recognized as a vital source of power by states. As such, rather than simply trying to curtail platforms' growth, states seek to govern *through* platforms: to instrumentalize and mobilize them in pursuit of geostrategic objectives. At the same time, in a world characterized by competition and growing calls for platform regulation, home state backing is becoming indispensable for US and Chinese platform firms to maintain and expand the dominance of their digital ecosystems in the global political economy. It is this increasingly symbiotic relationship between states and platform firms that we refer to as *state platform capitalism* (SPC).

We conceptualize SPC as the collaborative and reinforcing individual efforts of states and platform firms – principally in the United States and China – to compete to establish and maintain control over the technology stacks that serve as the underlying infrastructure of globalization. The power exercised by digital platforms derives from their technical and corporate control over the computational infrastructures and business ecosystems upon which a growing share of global economic activity depends. For states, platforms represent potential 'points of infrastructural control [which] can serve as proxies to regain (or gain) control or manipulate the flow of money, information, and the marketplace of ideas in the digital sphere' (Musiani et al., 2016, 4). Control over the technology stacks and socio-economic exchanges which platforms orchestrate is central the competitive dynamics of SPC. Given the ongoing expansion of states' definitions of 'national security' and the geopolitical competition for network centrality, it is unsurprising that platforms have become central to great power rivalry between the United States and China (Gray, 2021; Shen and He, 2022).

Most major digital platform firms are domiciled in either the United States or China, and both states are deploying a barrage of state capitalist practices to establish control over digital platforms and enlist them in pursuit of geostrategic objectives. Three distinctive competition dynamics result, which we outline here in turn as: *infrastructural platform geopolitics, digital dependencies,* and *cross-stack rivalry.*

Infrastructural platform geopolitics has emerged as states have come to recognize the extraterritorial power potentials of transnational infrastructures (Westermeier, 2020; Abels and Bieling, 2024), while platforms have increasing taken on infrastructural properties (Plantin et al., 2018; Shen, 2022a). Some platform firms can be directly *weaponized* (Farrell and Newman, 2023) by their host states in nakedly geopolitical ways. For instance, WikiLeaks was famously denied vital services by internet platforms such as Amazon Web Services, and EveryDNS at the behest of US government pressure (Tusikov, 2021), while the second Trump administration has ordered a ban on access to US chip design platforms for Chinese firms. However, for the time being, such weaponization remains the exception rather than the norm, and this tremendous power to deny adversaries access to (or otherwise weaponize) platforms remains latent. Indeed, excessive weaponization initiatives are likely to reduce the appeal of platforms and induce users to switch to other platforms despite the cost. Instead, platforms' infrastructural power derives from how they entrench power relations by monopolizing key passage points, while rerouting, ordering, and governing flows of data and capital in ways which potentially redound to the benefit of their home states (Westermeier, 2020; Bakonyi and Darwich, 2024; Hardaker, 2025). To this end, states seek to secure favourable regulatory environments (both at home and abroad), preferential financing, and forms of strategic endorsement that enable platforms to both scale and embed themselves in technology stacks.

This leads us to the second dynamic: fostering *digital dependencies.* Many countries are increasingly dependent upon US and Chinese platforms since they underpin access to the global economy (Mayer and Lu, 2025). Maintaining this dominant position is key to the profit strategies of platform firms, and it upholds the power asymmetries between states. Through lobbying, financial support, and implanting platforms with in bilateral agreements and initiatives, states seek to render third countries' technology stacks critically reliant upon their platform infrastructures and embed them in overseas technology stacks. At the same time, states and platforms collaborate to centralize and police access to the critical resources which sustain their dominance – including compute power (as in licensing regimes for NVIDIA accelerator chips and remote AI datacentre access) and data flows (especially for AI model training). Limiting interoperability and resisting multihoming by third countries are key targets for platforms' home states in fostering digital dependencies.

Finally, and as discussed further in the next section, states and platforms collectively practise forms of *cross-stack rivalry*. Platforms compete as sprawling business ecosystems rather than price or quality of individual product lines. This can limit rivalry and competition between platforms from the same home state, giving rise to 'frenemy' relations or coopetition between platforms (Gupta et al., 2025). States may support the emergence of such cooperative relations in overseas markets in efforts to cohere third countries into the national technology stack of the United States or China. Platforms' extraterritorial expansion may be supported by such a state-facilitated *bundling* of functions, as in shared investments in data centres, cabling systems, or other infrastructure that comprises digital stacks. Moreover, cooperative relations mean successful competition in one field (such as an overseas cloud market) is likely to redound to the benefit of platforms from the same home state.

None of this is to say that the interests of big tech platforms and home states are entirely aligned. They sometimes diverge and are subject to contestation and renegotiation. Platforms cannot be reduced to mere instruments of political power. Indeed, it is precisely because 'platform ecosystems are not simply commercial mechanisms or state-controlled entities . . . [that] they are becoming more and more part of a global geopolitical contest' (van Dijck and Lin, 2022, 65). In the following sections, we inquire more deeply into the specific mechanisms which drive platforms and states to cooperate in the global competition for digital dominance.

3 The US Stack

3.1 Introduction

In 2022, Eric Schmidt, former CEO of Google, issued a stark warning from a podium at the Capital Hilton Hotel in Washington DC. The United States risked falling behind China in the digital technology race:

> It's possible to imagine a dark future . . . Imagine that everything around you, everything you see in this room, has a component of Chinese values in it . . . free speech being restricted, being recorded, being surveilled. While China

has achieved many impressive things, I would not want to live there ... The real issue here is that we screwed up. We cannot get '5Ged' again. I was part of the errors 20 years ago and 30 years ago in the semiconductor sector, where we collectively thought, 'That's fine, that's not that important, we can figure it out, globalization will work.' Meanwhile, we've ended up in a situation where my phone doesn't work most of the time, whereas in China, where I may or may not be allowed back into, they have roughly a billion people on track to having a gigabit to their mobile phones in urban centers within the next year or two. (Schmidt, 2022)

Schmidt was launching his new initiative, the Special Competitive Studies Project (SCSP). Explicitly modelled on Henry Kissinger's 'Special Studies Project', the Rockefeller-funded bipartisan initiative which built public consent and enthusiasm for the massive military and technology investments needed to prosecute the Cold War, Schmidt's SCSP would bring together leading industry figures and politicians to cement the consensus for public investments in digital technologies to counter the 'China challenge'. He emphasized that the 'unifying idea of SCSP is competition, both within the various players in our system and between countries. This competition makes us stronger, not weaker. We need to win that competition' (Schmidt, 2022).

Schmidt's close collaboration with the Biden administration came to an end with the return of Donald Trump to the White House. But the personal intimacy between big tech leaders and state managers did not. The front row of Donald Trump's presidential inauguration at St John's Episcopal Church in January 2025 was reserved for Google CEO Sundar Pichai, Meta CEO Mark Zuckerberg, Apple CEO Tim Cook, Amazon's Jeff Bezos, and Tesla CEO Elon Musk – a clear signal of the privileged access to the levers of statehood to be granted to platform leaders. This section charts the central role of platform firms in driving the US global digital technology dominance, before examining how the state and platform firms are increasingly collaborating to defend this dominance in the face of growing Chinese competition.

3.2 The US Stack

The United States is home to the world's most dynamic technology sector, whose firms dominate all nearly all key layers of the technology stack. Chip designer NVIDIA's market capitalization is roughly equivalent to the top-forty publicly listed German firms, while Microsoft's exceeds the entire FTSE 100 (Nikou Asgari et al., 2024). The United States has spawned the world's largest platforms, whose global footprint is so ubiquitous that by some accounts it constitutes a form of 'digital colonialism' in its relations with other countries

(Kwet, 2019). Moreover, the US tech sector is deepening its ties with the American state (González, 2024). Platform firms are central to this trend.

Leading platform firms that emerged from Silicon Valley's high-technology ecosystem began to develop increasingly close ties with the US government during the war on terror after 2001 (Weiss, 2014; O'Mara, 2020). Their relationship encompasses both widespread government contracting and an emphasis on public-private partnerships (PPPs) (Weiss and Thurbon, 2020). Federal institutions such as the National Science Foundation, NASA, DARPA, the SBA, and National Labs dole out substantial funding in support of research and development that is critical to the US digital economy (Mazzucato, 2013; Wade, 2017; Tassinari, 2018). Despite this financial support, however, US techno-industrial policy remains relatively decentralized – and rather than directly intervening and 'picking winners', policy is designed to steer and support innovation. Allen et al. (2022, 22) describe this as a 'large, decentralized apparatus for innovation within the US federal government, in which scores of agencies, often working in a largely uncoordinated fashion, engage with private firms to promote innovative breakthroughs in a wide array of sectors'. While each of these agencies has independent priorities, an underlying but emergent strategy is increasingly discernible. The US government seeks to safeguard the dominant position of its platforms worldwide, while progressively incorporating them into the military-industrial complex, because they possess unique attributes that, when mobilized, augment long-term geostrategic objectives.

Military and national security interests consequently play an outsized role allocating funding in this uncoordinated funding environment. US capital markets continue to be the world's largest and most liquid, accounting for around 40% of the world's total equities (around four times that of China). Wall Street established powerful conduits in Silicon Valley VC during the 1990s and cemented the route to IPO via the NASDAQ, developing links between financial and tech capital have only grown in scope and scale since (Walker, 2006). Smaller tech firms enjoy uniquely abundant private capital markets, while Wall Street offers vast liquidity for IPOs or buyouts. But the influence of the US national security state looms large. Schwartz (2017, 327) describes it as a 'vast technology enterprise spanning R&D, seed funding, commercialization, and both spin-off and spin-on of new technologies'. Private capital commonly follows in the wake of big bets placed on unlisted technology firms by the Department of Defense, since receiving funding from the US national security state (or one of its financial conduits) acts as a seal of approval for investors. These dynamics explain how, as Robinson (2020, 40) explains, the 'Silicon Valley-Wall Street nexus becomes in turn interlocked with the military-industrial-security complex'.

There is a long history of cooperation between the US government and American defence contractors. Yet the increasingly intimate relationships between elites in Washington and Silicon Valley, and dense financial links between public and private entities in the tech sector, represent a qualitative shift in the way that nominally civilian firms are integrated into security procurement. The US government not only offers financial resources, but it has also expanded control over tech firms – and platform firms in particular – through state capitalist regulatory instruments that are justified by the threat posed by China (Gertz and Evers, 2020). For instance, the Trump administration's national cyber strategy published in 2018 labelled China a 'strategic competitor', concluding that the 'vitality of the American marketplace and American innovation' in the tech sector is a matter of national security (The White House, 2018, 14). The strategy envisions a symbiotic relationship between the state – namely its defence-related organizations – and American tech firms. This was echoed by the DoD's (U.S. Department of Defense, 2018, 9) *Cyber Strategy*, which, in short, is designed to:

> defend forward, shape the day-to-day competition, and prepare for war by building a more lethal force, expanding alliances and partnerships, reforming the Department, and cultivating talent, while actively competing against and deterring our competitors. Taken together, these mutually reinforcing activities will enable the Department to compete, deter, and win in the cyberspace domain.

Platform firms have become an important pillar of national security strategy because they provide vital infrastructural and technological services which state agencies do not possess, while their R&D budgets dwarf available public resources and incumbent defence contractors. The Defense Innovation Unit reported that US platform giants outspend its top defence contractors (e.g., Lockheed Martin and Raytheon) on R&D by 11-to-1 (Brown, 2021, 13). Google's 2024 R&D spending amounted to $45 bn, around five times the budget of the National Science Foundation. Collaboration offers state agencies the opportunity to influence platforms' R&D strategies, as in the National Cyber Strategy that will 'use its purchasing power' to shape innovation and influence firm behaviour in support of defence goals (The White House, 2018, 8). The 'third offset' – a military strategy aiming to leverage private sector innovations for defence purposes – became embedded in the 2018 *National Defense Strategy* (Gentile et al., 2021). Ultimately the military-industrial-security complex is in the process of reworking state-business relations in the platform sector, with the objective of aligning the business strategies of the world's largest platform firms with Washington's geostrategic imperatives.

One objective of state financial support is to support the incorporation of platform and other high-tech firms into the defence sector. This requires more than an alignment of financial interests, and explains the growing integration between political and tech elites in Washington and Silicon Valley. For example, the Defense Innovation Board (DIB) was established in 2016, bringing together leaders from the private tech sector, venture capitalists and former military officers who advise the Department of Defense on its technology policy. Its first chair was Eric Schmidt. The DIB (Defense Innovation Board, 2024) explains:

> Peer and near-peer competitors are challenging U.S. primacy across a number of domains and technologies, and DoD must navigate shifting economic and industry environments to meet these challenges and achieve mission success. In this context, the DIB provides outside independent expertise to the Department to support the warfighter and encourage innovative best practices throughout the armed forces.

The DIB's mirror image in the private sector is the America's Frontier Fund (AFF). AFF is a tech-focused venture capital outfit, whose website announced that:

> The time to act is now. We are in a great-power competition, and the United States is falling behind. By 2030, we risk losing our edge in microelectronics, AI, 5 G, and quantum to our adversaries. At a time when technology advantage is strategic advantage, this is not a risk we can take. (America's Frontier Fund, 2022)

The AFF can boast tech, financial and governmental elites among its employees. Its Board of Directors has included former Secretary of Defense Ash Carter and retired Lieutenant General H. R. McMaster, while its current CEO Gilman Louie previously served as the CEO of IQT (formerly In-Q-Tel), a public venture capital firm established in 1999 by the CIA and other US government agencies that receives well over $100 m annually in tax revenue. IQT itself 'focuses on the 15,000+ early stage venture-backed startup companies in the U.S. and select other countries' (IQT, 2024).

Sustained efforts by both sides to integrate digital technologies with the US military explains the explosion of government contracts with Amazon, Google, Microsoft, Facebook, and Twitter since 2017.[2] The CIA signed an initial $600 m contract with Amazon Web Services (AWS) in 2013, and awarded a decade-long contract worth 'tens of billions of dollars' to AWS, Microsoft Azure, IBM, Google, and Oracle in 2020 for cloud computing services (Konkel, 2020). Similarly, the National Security Agency (NSA) inked a US$10 bn contract

---

[2] See https://bigtechsellswar.com/.

with Amazon in 2021 for cloud computing services (Gregg, 2021). Google has developed collaborative relationships with the CIA, US Navy, and Air Force as it develops a bid for the Joint Warfighter Cloud Capability contract with the Pentagon (Simonite, 2021). And the NSA (2022) recently established a Cybersecurity Collaboration Center it describes as a 'groundbreaking hub for engagement with the private sector ... to create an environment for information sharing between NSA and its partners combining our respective expertise, techniques, and capabilities to secure the nation's most critical networks ... [representing] a vital part of a whole-of-nation approach to cybersecurity'.

3.3 The American Pivot

Until recently, the United States largely pursued a 'free' global digital trade regime which upheld the dominance of its platforms globally. However, Donald Trump's message that free trade represented a cost to the US economy has since come to form a cross-party consensus on the need for mercantilist practices, especially in the digital sphere. The Biden administration committed to protecting strategic sectors within a proverbial 'small yard' by a 'high fence' that includes export controls, investment screening, and tariffs (Sullivan, 2022). Such initiatives signal a broad shift in US policy, in which the global and systemic significance of US digital platforms is recognized – and safeguarding their overwhelming power is an explicit objective requiring direct and explicit forms of intervention anathema to a free trade agenda. In addition to discouraging other governments from regulating US platform firms, this is done by limiting Chinese platform firms' access to capital, technology, and markets.

The Clean Network Initiative (Table 2) was introduced by the Trump administration, and it represented the first major rupture in the field of digital policy. Whereas previous policy underpinned globalization and prioritized free trade, the Clean Network Initiative discouraged governments and firms from working with 'high-risk' Chinese firms such as Huawei and ZTE that are purportedly 'required to comply with directives of the Chinese Communist Party' (U.S. State Department, 2021). Six fields of regulation were identified, whose collective ambition was to 'clean' the technology stacks of third countries of Chinese operators.

The results of the Clean Network Initiative were mixed. While it attracted broad formal support, fewer countries were prepared to make the hard trade-offs involved in ending relations with Chinese firms. A number of countries did cease doing business with Huawei: Canada commissioned Ericsson, Nokia and Samsung to build its 5 G networks, while the UK banned the installation of new Huawei equipment in 2020 and plans to remove it entirely by 2027 (Payne and

Table 2 Six components of the Clean Network introduced by US Secretary of State Mike Pompeo (from U.S. Dept. of State, 2020)

Component	Description
Clean Carrier	To ensure that People's Republic of China (PRC) carriers are not connected with US telecommunications networks. Such companies pose a danger to US national security and should not provide international telecommunications services to and from the United States.
Clean Store	To remove untrusted applications from US mobile app stores. PRC apps threaten our privacy, proliferate viruses, censor content, and spread propaganda and disinformation. Americans' most sensitive personal and business information must be protected on their mobile phones from exploitation and theft for the CCP's benefit.
Clean Apps	To prevent untrusted PRC smartphone manufacturers from pre-installing – or otherwise making available for download – trusted apps on their apps store. Huawei, an arm of the PRC surveillance state, is trading on the innovations and reputations of leading US and foreign companies. These companies should remove their apps from Huawei's app store to ensure they are not partnering with a human rights abuser.
Clean Cloud	To prevent US citizens' most sensitive personal information and our businesses' most valuable intellectual property, including COVID-19 vaccine research, from being stored and processed on cloud-based systems accessible to our foreign adversaries through companies such as Alibaba, Baidu, China Mobile, China Telecom, and Tencent.
Clean Cable	To ensure the undersea cables connecting our country to the global internet are not subverted for intelligence gathering by the PRC at hyper scale. We will also work with foreign partners to ensure that undersea cables around the world aren't similarly subject to compromise.
Clean Path	The 5 G Clean Path is an end-to-end communication path that does not use any transmission, control, computing, or storage equipment from untrusted IT vendors, such as Huawei and ZTE, which are required to comply with directives of the Chinese Communist Party.

Fildes, 2020). While it impacted Huawei's global operations, it failed to deal the Chinese firm a mortal blow. Huawei has since recovered and even strengthened its competitive position across a widening range of product categories and services. But despite mixed results, the Clean Network undeniably altered the course of US policy.

The Biden administration formally shelved the Clean Network Initiative, but it largely maintained and expanded the intent behind the Trump-era policy regarding technology diplomacy. The CHIPS Act,[3] the Biden administration's flagship technology sector initiative subsidizing domestic semiconductor production, includes 'strong guardrails, ensuring that recipients do not build certain facilities in China and other countries of concern' (The White House, 2022a). These guardrails dovetail with a welter of new export controls aimed to starve Chinese platform giants of the advanced chips and manufacturing technologies necessary for their development of advanced networking equipment, smartphones, and AI (Ryan and Burman, 2024).

While the business strategies of US tech firms were once premised on access to both the United States and China, the CHIPS Act and associated US policymaking increasingly forces firms to choose. Meta, Google, Apple, Amazon, and Microsoft all recorded lobbying interest over the CHIPS Act (Bordelon and Oprysko, 2023) and have shown little hostility to other measures towards containing China's technology sector. US platforms are, as observed, heavily limited their ability to do business in China, while they often regard the revenue loss from such measures as a price worth paying to damage Chinese competitors. Indeed, firms seem prepared to go beyond the letter of the law. In May 2024, Microsoft announced it was offering 700–800 members of staff at its flagship Research Asia AI centre in Beijing relocation to the United States and elsewhere (Huang and Kubota, 2024).

In addition to supporting domestic semiconductor production, the United States seeks to inhibit Chinese firms from securing strategic positions in an increasingly substantial portion of the global digital ecosystem. Perhaps most notably, Washington has signalled that it would like to establish a regional trade deal that would inhibit the operations of Chinese platforms, particularly in Asia. The much-vaunted Indo-Pacific Strategy unveiled in February 2022 committed the United States to:

> [P]romote secure and trustworthy digital infrastructure, particularly cloud and telecommunications vendor diversity, including through innovative network architectures such as Open RAN by encouraging at-scale commercial

---

[3] The full title is the CHIPS and Science Act 2022 (see: www.congress.gov/bill/117th-congress/house-bill/4346/text).

deployments and cooperation on testing, such as through shared access to test beds to enable common standards development. We will also deepen shared resilience in critical government and infrastructure networks, while building new regional initiatives to improve collective cybersecurity and rapidly respond to cyber incidents. (The White House, 2022b, 17)

A strategy document leaked by *AXIOS* news agency in January 2021 revealed the existence of a China Strategy Group, co-chaired by Eric Schmidt and Jared Cohen (Hillary Clinton adviser), that produced a series of recommendations to the incoming Biden administration to restrain Chinese tech ascendancy (Allen-Ebrahimian, 2021). These included developing a 'new plurilateral coalition of "techno-democracies" to strengthen cooperation' and 'protect and preserve key areas of competitive technological advantage'. It further proposed an 'International Technology Finance Corporation ... to extend loans and loan guarantees to developing nations for tech infrastructure buildout consistent with liberal values, to counter the Digital Silk Road', alongside a 'Global Body for Standard-Setting' and 'multilateral trust zones to achieve global integration that promotes American values'. The objective was to 'incentivize collective innovation against China in AI, quantum computing, 5 G, etc ... To gain access to the benefits of the Trust Zone, countries would have to commit to a Huawei-free zone'.

The Biden and second Trump administrations have transformed a considerable part of the China Strategy Group's recommendations into policy. Initiatives have proliferated, from the addition of Chinese technology firms to the US (restricted) Entity List and the expansion of export controls (many of which impact third countries via the Foreign Direct Product Rule), to inbound and outbound investment screening mechanisms, and a punitive licensing regime for semiconductors, AI, and access to compute (Sastry et al., 2024). Measures have also targeted particular firms. Along with platform giants Huawei and ZTE, AI firm DeepSeek has attracted a range of punitive measures following the release of its breakthrough R1 model – including CFIUS reviews, bans on public procurement and use by government personnel, and the potential ban of its app from Apple and Android stores. Meanwhile, the Trump administration signalled its support for domestic US platforms by co-ordinating the $500 bn Stargate investment, a project to build AI datacentres within the United States funded by a private sector consortium led by OpenAI, SoftBank, Oracle, and UAE-based MGX, while repealing AI safety regulations. And Trump inked well over $200 bn in major deals for the proliferation of AI data centres involving OpenAI, NVIDIA, Amazon, and others on a tour of the Middle East in May 2025 (Ghosh, 2025).

Platforms are at the centre of US geostrategic objectives because, on one hand, they integrate the various components of the technology stack, while, on the other hand, they carve out digital ecosystems in which they can establish and enforce rules which bolster the global power of the United States. The United States uses subsidies and lucrative contracts to incorporate platform firms into the defence and national security sectors, while encouraging firms to bolster its geostrategic objectives. It also discourages its platform firms from engaging with their Chinese counterparts. Meanwhile it seeks to deny Chinese firms access to expertise, capital, and markets. To this end, the United States encourages other countries to establish exclusive relationships with US-based platform firms at the expense of their existing relations with Chinese tech firms. US platform firms have been willing, and in many cases eager, collaborators to these ends. The US variant of state platform capitalism is geared towards the construction and maintenance of a geographically extensive 'national stack' – devoid of Chinese technology – that progressively expands its role as supreme mediator of socio-economic relations worldwide.

4 The Chinese Stack

4.1 Introduction

China is home to the only concentration of globally significant internet giants outside of the United States (Table 3). Firms such as Alibaba, Tencent, Baidu, and Huawei are principally domestically focused, and form part of a technology stack with a considerable degree of operational autonomy from US platform services. But China's platforms increasingly operate with the aim of internationalizing their operations, and they are the closest that US platforms have to global rivals. This section charts the integration of Chinese platform firms' entanglements with the party-state, and the resultant emergence of a variety of state platform capitalism, before exploring how state and corporate motives align in Chinese platforms' internationalization drive.

4.2 Private Power?

Until recently, some viewed China's digital platform economy as a potential bastion of private economic and political power that could even potentially challenge the authority of the party-state (Tse, 2015). After all, China's digital giants emerged in the shadows of the state economy, driven less by central planning or state subsidies, but by innovative and often ruthless entrepreneurialism in a fiercely competitive domestic market (Fannin, 2019). Moreover, despite regularly attending Party Congresses and otherwise being connected with the upper echelons of China's political elite, China's new breed of tech

Table 3 China's platform giants

Platform	Operations	Market capitalization (Q1 2024)/most recent valuation (bn $US)	Revenue (2023) (bn $US)
Tencent	Social Media, fintech, e-commerce, gaming, AI	373	86
ByteDance	Social media (Douyin/TikTok), news (Jinri Toutiao)	268	120
Alibaba Group	E-commerce (Taobao, Tmall), cloud computing, logistics (Cainiao)	178	131
Pinduoduo	E-commerce	166	35
Huawei*	Smartphones, OS, network equipment	139	92
Meituan	Food delivery	82	39
Ant group	Fintech	79	16**
Shein (XiYin)***	Retail, logistics	66	45
NetEase	Gaming and music	63	15
Xiaomi	Smartphones, smart devices, IoT	51	38
JD.com	E-commerce, logistics	42	153
Baidu	Search, Video (iQiyi), AI	36	19
Trip.com	Travel	31	6
Kuaishou	Video	28	16
DiDi Global	Ride-hailing	22	27
Bilibili	Live streaming	5	3
Weibo	Social media	2	2
Kingsoft	Software, cloud services, gaming	0.6	1

Source: Authors, financial data from *S&P Capital IQ Pro* and media reports
* Huawei figures are loose estimates for 2022 from Hurun (2022).
** Data for 2022.
*** Shein sales figures are loose estimates from the Financial Times McMorrow et al. (2024).

entrepreneurs cultivated an air of distance from the party-state. Their messaging, media and fintech apps were largely not integrated with extant state-owned systems, and seemed to point towards the weakening of state monopoly control of strategic sectors like banking and media.

Any such notions were dramatically dispelled in the autumn of 2020. Ant Financial – a spinoff of Alibaba specializing in fintech services – was due to be dual-listed on the Shanghai and Hong Kong stock exchanges on November 5. Ant's IPO generated huge excitement amongst investors, and was to represent the world's largest ever (with a predicted valuation of $313 bn). A week beforehand, however, Jack Ma (Alibaba and Ant founder) delivered a potent speech to assorted bankers and party-state officials at the Shanghai Bund Forum. He attacked China's state-dominated financial system, which he accused of having a 'pawnshop mentality'. He lamented that there are 'no systemic financial risks in China because there's no financial system in China', emphasizing the country's strict regulations on private lending (Collier, 2022, 2). Ma proposed opening the financial sector to digital platforms, with big data to be used as a source of trust rather than traditional collateral (exactly what Ant set out to achieve with its AliPay system). The response from the party-state was swift. Two days before the IPO was due to proceed, the Shanghai Stock Exchange posted a notice suspending the IPO due to disclosure issues. Rumour had it that Xi Jinping had intervened directly.

The year that followed witnessed a dramatic 'regulatory storm', as interventions tore through the business operations of China's digital giants (Naughton, 2021). Tencent, Alibaba, and Meituan faced antitrust fines surrounding their sprawling acquisition strategies and engagements with suppliers. Tencent also suffered the consequences (alongside rival NetEase) of a crackdown on young people's video gaming habits. Education platforms offering for-profit tutoring services were banned outright. And major players in the transport service platform sector such as Didi and Full Truck Alliance faced protracted scrutiny over their cybersecurity and export of user data. The storm culminated in the world's first regulatory frameworks for recommendation algorithms and generative AI.

The regulatory storm hit China's highly valued platform firm stocks hard, contributing to the broader wipeout of $6 trillion from Chinese equities from 2021–4 (Vishnoi and Yang, 2024). But even more significantly, it laid bare how deeply China's platform economy was both exposed to and imbricated with the Chinese state (To, 2023). Such dramatic and public interventions against large private-sector firms had previously been rare in China, where subtler methods of ensuring political acquiescence were typically favoured – and regulators thought to lack the toolkit necessary to effectively corral private enterprise to pursue political ends (Collier, 2022). This regulatory overhaul precipitated a new era in which high technology was increasingly put 'in service of the state' (Segal, 2018).

4.3 Entanglements with the State

Despite their Silicon Valley–inspired language and branding, China's platforms had never been simple products of the 'free market', or evidence of 'entrepreneurial spirits' chafing under the pressures of a bureaucratic state. Rather, they owed their very existence to the Chinese party-state's extensive and powerful internet content regulations. American internet firms entering the Chinese market during the late 1990s and early 2000s typically did not face formal exclusions, and were generally allowed to operate in markets where incumbents largely did not exist. However, they did encounter a thicket of regulations and licensing requirements which made doing business considerably more difficult than in most jurisdictions. Alongside cultural and language barriers, this meant their adoption was very slow – which eventually allowed local rivals to steal a march on US internet giants (Mueller and Farhat, 2022).

From the late 2000s, China began to block access to sites like YouTube, Google, Facebook, and Twitter in response to concerns over foreign penetration of China's otherwise strictly regulated media ecosystem. These bans dealt a succession of blows to US-based platform firms' efforts to operate in China, leaving the field clear for China's domestic internet firms to consolidate control over the domestic market. For instance, Baidu was able to quintuple its revenues in the year after Google's withdrawal from China in 2009 (McKnight et al., 2023, 248–252). The rocky terrain of China's internet economy and the state's efforts to block foreign media content collectively amounted to an accidental infant industry protection policy for its nascent platform companies (Foster and Azmeh, 2020). The outcome was a curious kind of 'Galapagos effect' that allowed indigenous Chinese platforms that were largely disconnected from the US-centred stack to grow rapidly (Bratton, 2018).

The relatively late development of China's internet infrastructure further enabled Chinese firms to pursue leapfrog development strategies (Li et al., 2018; Davis and Xiao, 2021). Most consumers bypassed desktop and laptop computers altogether. Already by 2014, 90% of Chinese accessed the web via mobile rather than desktop devices. As such, Chinese platform firms optimized their business processes and technical designs for smartphone systems in ways which US platforms (which had legacy desktop-optimized versions) found challenging, giving them a substantive advantage on home terrain.

Restricting foreign firms' operations did not undermine competition. Intense domestic rivalries drove Chinese internet firms to adopt adaptable and innovative business strategies (Zeng and Glaister, 2016). Their vast local base of operations – with over one billion internet users to date – offered opportunities to compete for users, innovate, and ultimately hone highly effective business strategies. For example, lax regulatory oversight (including a virtual absence of private sector competition policy) encouraged these companies to develop sprawling cross-equity holdings of smaller firms across multiple product lines (Jia and Winseck, 2018). China's platforms increasingly exhibit the horizontal integration characteristic of East Asian business groups such as *keiretsu* and *chaebol* (Jia et al., 2018) – with Alibaba Group offering services in e-commerce, social media, fintech, cloud computing and electric vehicles, for instance. China's app economy is characterized by 'superapps' such as Tencent-owned WeChat – multifunctional platforms which integrate social media, digital payments and fintech, with services such as booking cabs and making restaurant reservations. Network and lock-in effects have cemented the role of these platforms in China's digital ecosystem.

Around the mid-2010s, policymakers recognized the critical and developmental potential of digital technologies. Since then, China's digital platform economy has become folded into this China's techno-nationalist developmental strategy (Jia, 2021; Zhang and Lan, 2023) – an increasingly comprehensive set of industrial policies dubbed by economist Barry Naughton (2020b, 82) as the 'greatest single commitment of government resources to an industrial policy objective in history'.

State capitalist practices target platforms in several ways. China's digital platforms increasingly fulfil key institutional functions delegated by state agencies. Government services are increasingly delivered through PPPs that involve platform firms (Ma et al., 2023). For instance, WeChat provides a growing range of essential administrative services such as digital identification cards, access to urban medical booking portals, and health codes during the COVID-19 pandemic. Didi systematically shares data with urban authorities to assist in transport planning and management (Chan and Kwok, 2022). And Shanghai's mapping and food delivery platforms are delegated responsibility and authority to regulate food hygiene standards by the municipal government (Chan and Kwok, 2024).

These PPP arrangements have, in some cases, developed into full-blown 'state-commercial complexes' (Liu, 2024a). Alibaba Group's construction of a data centre for Guizhou province's government was initiated by the provincial and central governments in 2014. Within months, Alibaba Cloud's engineers had constructed a cloud system at no monetary cost to the provincial government. In exchange, Guizhou offered exclusive access to its vast reservoir of administrative data which Alibaba Cloud could analyse and capitalize. It also provided privileged opportunities for Alibaba's Taobao to develop e-commerce infrastructures in the province's rural areas. Alibaba's role in Guizhou was subsequently given national-level endorsement as a key node in the 2022 National Integrated Big Data Centre System (NIBDCS), which aims to build an integrated national system of administrative data.

Contracting practices are systematized into broader techno-nationalist development strategies, in which platform firms are assigned roles as national champions. For instance, China's National Development and Reform Commission approved investment plans for a range of tech giants in mid-2023 (Tang and Nulimaimaiti, 2023). This paved the way for them to access substantial state resources, including an anticipated $139 bn worth of government bond-financed funding directed towards developing 'new productive forces' in advanced technologies (including big data and AI) (Pomfret et al., 2024). Under the 2017 'AI New Generation Artificial Intelligence Development Plan', fifteen firms were afforded key roles in developing open AI platforms for specific industrial purposes. These included Baidu (autonomous vehicles), Alibaba Group (smart cities), Tencent (medical imaging), and iFlyTek (natural language processing) (Larsen, 2019; Roberts et al., 2021). Designated firms are afforded access to privileged state financial and data resources (Horowitz et al., 2018) which aligns state developmental objectives with profit incentives for platforms. Baidu, for instance, was able to successfully leverage its role as a AI Open Innovation Platform provider to develop its Apollo autonomous driving platform – attracting third-party firms such as BYD (Ren, 2022), and leveraging its position to become a major provider of autonomous driving ride-hailing services.[4] Its software is open access and available for collaborators and rivals to both build on and develop. Partly due to this concerted techno-industrial policy drive, China now significantly leads the United States in AI patents filings (Bloomberg News, 2023).

National security is a crucial component of China's techno-nationalist development plans. Platform firms play an important role in augmenting China's military capabilities, through its 'military-civil fusion' (MCF) efforts to incorporate private-sector innovations into previously state-dominated military procurement (White and Yu, 2023). By one estimate $68.5 bn of state financing has been deployed on MCF projects from 2015 to 2019, with evidence that Alibaba, Tencent, and Baidu have collaborated with Chinese military institutions (Kania

---

[4] BYD subsequently broke its contract with Baidu/Apollo to work towards establishing its own autonomous driving software.

and Laskai, 2021). For example, the Joint Laboratory for Intelligent Command and Control Technologies was established by Baidu and the state-owned defence firm China Electronics Technology Group (CETC), and its aim is to upgrade the Chinese military's information warfare capabilities (Creemers, 2019). Military contracts are simply the tip of a much larger iceberg. China's radically expanded conception of national security prioritizes substantive cooperation from its digital platform firms over individual data protection rights (Bradford, 2023) – from surveillance practices (Huang and Tsai, 2022) to consumer safety regulations (Martens and Zhao, 2021). China's government has also directed state-owned enterprises to replace US enterprise software with Chinese equivalents by 2027 through its secretive 'Delete America' directive (Lin, 2024).

China's platform economy is further characterized by a state-directed form of financialization (Jia and Winseck, 2018). Despite the legacy of the 2021 regulatory crackdown, China's platforms still enjoy high valuations. To the consternation of some American politicians, US investors have been and remain major financiers of China's digital technology firms (see Table 4), while US IPOs remain the goal of many Chinese platforms. China's highly open investment regime has enabled US investors (especially institutions) to take major stakes in these firms (Shen, 2020).

Despite their nominal private and global ownership, Chinese platforms also remain to a considerable degree under the effective control of China's party-state. Foreign investment into restricted sectors like telecoms is channelled through Variable Interest Entity (VIE) structures, where overseas investors hold shares in offshore shell companies rather than direct equity in the Chinese operating firms. VIE structures bypass foreign ownership prohibitions but operate in a legal grey area within China. Crucially, they grant foreigners limited voting rights, concentrating control with domestic founders and investors. The party-state maintains decisive leverage through regulation, licensing, embedded Party influence, and the ever-present threat of enforcement actions – helping to ensuring platforms align with state objectives regardless of their ownership structure (Chen, 2022).

Government guidance funds (GGFs), which deploy a mixture of state and private capital towards strategic goals, are another important tool. GGFs (including the prominent state-operated China Internet Investment Fund) controlled over $1.5 trillion in capital in 2021 (Wei et al., 2023). Capital steered by government guidance funds is deployed overwhelmingly to the technology sector. While a majority is invested in hardware development (especially semiconductor components), at least 17% is invested in software and computer services-based projects. Thanks to enormous investments in

Table 4 Tencent's top-20 owners, April 2024

Holder	Common Shares Outstanding (%)	Country	Owner Type
Naspers Ltd.	25.43	South Africa	Corporations (public)
Huateng Ma Co-Founder, Chairman & CEO	7.63	China	Individuals/insiders
Vanguard Group Inc.	2.68	USA	Traditional investment managers
BlackRock Inc.	2.3	USA	Traditional investment managers
Norges Bank Investment Management	1.11	Norway	Banks/investment banks
Ma Huateng Global Foundation	1.02	China	Charitable foundations
Capital Research and Management Co.	0.83	USA	Traditional investment Managers
JP Morgan Asset Management	0.81	USA	Traditional investment managers
E Fund Management Co. Ltd.	0.79	China	Traditional investment managers
FMR LLC	0.72	USA	Traditional investment managers
Baillie Gifford & Co.	0.63	United Kingdom	Traditional investment managers
State Street Global Advisors Inc.	0.54	USA	Traditional investment managers

Table 4 (cont.)

Holder	Common Shares Outstanding (%)	Country	Owner Type
Invesco Ltd.	0.44	USA	Traditional investment managers
Fidelity International Ltd.	0.41	Bermuda	Traditional investment managers
UBS Asset Management AG	0.36	Switzerland	Traditional investment managers
Dimensional Fund Advisors LP	0.34	USA	Traditional investment managers
Geode Capital Management LLC	0.34	USA	Traditional investment managers
abrdn PLC	0.3	United Kingdom	Traditional investment managers
Canada Pension Plan Investment Board	0.29	Canada	Government pension sponsors
Massachusetts Financial Services Company	0.29	USA	Traditional investment managers

Source: S&P Capital IQ Pro

technology startups from GGFs, platform giants, and private (domestic and international) investors, China now rivals the United States in its share of global unicorn firms (unlisted startups valued at over $1 bn). In 2023, China produced 56 unicorns, second only to the US 70. Over one-third of Chinese startups were spun out of state-owned enterprises (Hurun, 2024).

The state also plays a role as direct (minority) owner of platform firms. Chinese state entities have taken 'golden shares' in a number firms like Alibaba, Tencent, and ByteDance. Alibaba recently disclosed that state funds had purchased such stakes in over twelve of its business entities (Zheng, 2024).

These specially issued shares, though nominally small, permit state agencies significant powers to nominate company directors or grant them privileged control over board-level decision-making processes. Even when not used directly, they are likely to restrict the independence of companies and offer insight into their operations for the party-state – by embedding cadres in privileged positions within big tech firms.

None of this is to say that the party-state enjoys total or unidirectional power over its platform sector. On the contrary, it remains deeply reliant upon the dynamism and innovation capabilities of the private economy. The 'regulatory storm' ultimately blew over in 2023, and Jack Ma was politically rehabilitated in February of 2025 when President Xi convened a forum with Chinese tech leaders (Zhang, 2025). The CEO of Hangzhou's DeepSeek – a private AI firm with few connections to the party-state which launched its DeepSeek-R1 large language model the month before – was also in attendance. Xi proclaimed his commitment to deploying the full resources of the state towards supporting the development of the new breed of AI models being developed or sponsored by China's technology firms at a Politburo study session in April 2025 (Xinhua, 2025).

4.4 Internationalization Drive

China's digital giants have made significant progress in their efforts to expand overseas. Four of the US top-ten most downloaded smartphone apps are Chinese owned (see Table 5). And Alibaba Group, for instance, derives over a third of its revenues from its international operations (Liu, 2024b). China's platform firms have profit motives firmly in mind when growing overseas operations. As Shen (2022b) writes, there exist 'complicated forms of power struggles among different government entities and units of internet capital across hardware, network and application layers'. Firms like Tencent and Alibaba compete directly with one another for market share in fields like cloud computing.

Rather than acting as a constraint on their competitiveness, engagement with the state provides critical support for Chinese platforms' efforts to internationalize their businesses. Key in this regard is the 'Digital Silk Road' (DSR), which was launched in 2017 as a component of the broader Belt and Road Initiative (BRI), and aims to consolidate, integrate, and expand the activities of China's platform firms in the name of international development objectives. The DSR is necessary precisely because most of what nominally constitute its activities are driven by the commercial decisions of private internet firms, rather than centrally co-ordinated by ministries or carried out by state actors.

Table 5 China's tech stack and its global expansion

Category	Industries	Key firms	Overseas markets and competition
Applications/ interfaces	e-Commerce, Smart City, Fintech, Social Media, gaming, commercial AI	Alibaba, Huawei, Tencent, private SMEs	Dominant in Southeast Asia and Africa, increasing global reach.
Cloud services	Cloud, Server, Data Centre Services	Huawei, Tencent, Alibaba	Strong in Southeast Asia and Middle East, small share (~5%) of global markets.
Digital devices	Phones, Tablets, PCs, Modems	Transsion, Oppo, Vivo, Xiaomi, DJI, XAG	Major players in emerging markets (including non-BRI countries like India).
Telecom infrastructure	3/4/5/6 G; Submarine, Terrestrial, and Satellite Connections	Huawei/HMN, ZTE, Inspur, China Mobile, Unicom, China Telecom, China Unicom	Compete with Nokia, Ericsson, and Samsung in emerging economies. Compete with US platform giants in undersea cabling. Compete with Vodafone, Telenor, Verizon, and AT&T in BRI countries, esp. Africa and Central Asia.
IT/Smart infrastructure	Smart energy projects like photovoltaic networks, virtual power plants; hardware and software for smart-city infrastructures	Alibaba, Huawei, ZTE, Hikvision, State Grid Corporation of China, smart-energy SMEs	Competing globally in smart city projects against Amazon, Microsoft, Google, ABB, Siemens, and GE.

Source: Authors, adapted from Triolo (2022) and Heeks et al. (2024)

The importance of the party-state's support for China's private internet giants should not be underestimated. China's platform firms mobilize the Digital Silk Road (DSR) like a franchise model, seeking to obtain official policy support for their profit-driven investment decisions (Triolo, 2022). China's telecoms firms are encouraged to invest directly in provisioning of hard infrastructure overseas as part of the BRI and DSR. Subject to soft budget constraints (by way of preferential access to state financing), they are consequently able to prioritize strategic objectives, such as expanding coverage at the expense of profits. Private firms operating at other layers of the stack (see Table 5) leverage Chinese state firms' significant cost advantages in providing hardware such as undersea cabling, 5/6 G base stations, and telecommunications networks. Contracts and financing for hard infrastructure often include conditions necessitating further spending with Chinese entities or simply are only interoperable with Chinese software providers – and so produce 'cross-layer dependencies' (Heeks et al., 2024). As such, multiple products and services are 'bundled' with one another, integrating Chinese firms across layers of a third country's technology stack.

China's state platform capitalism is perhaps most visible overseas in Southeast Asia, where Chinese platforms have expanded rapidly (Jia et al., 2018). Overseas Chinese populations with have provided a ready audience for Chinese e-commerce, social media, and digital payments platforms. And governments in the region often have few reservations about collaborating with Chinese firms – especially when major investments and favourable financing deals are on offer. In Malaysia, the state-backed Malaysia Digital Economy Corporation collaborated with Alibaba's Cainiao logistics platform and Lazada e-commerce system to develop a Digital Free Trade Zone (DFTZ) as part of a major Kuala Lumpur logistics cluster in 2017 (Naughton, 2020a). The DFTZ is the first major overseas project to incorporate the Ali-led electronic World Trade Platform (eWTP), a digital trade facilitation initiative initiated by Jack Ma endorsed by the 2016 G20 summit. Alibaba collaborated with Chinese ministerial heads to obtain permission for private provision of customs checks through online verification and clearance mechanisms in support of the DFTZ (Wang and Yu, 2022). A second eWTP-integrated zone went into operation in Thailand in 2022 (Cao, 2022). In Indonesia, Huawei and ZTE increasingly provide extensive physical networking infrastructure, software solutions and cybersecurity training packages to local and national governments (Priyandita et al., 2022). This has enabled and encouraged the entry of Chinese smartphone, fintech, and cloud players into Indonesia at scale (Rakhmat, 2022, He, 2024).

China's firms have expanded to challenge US incumbents because they offer vital digital infrastructures and services at highly competitive prices. This is especially so in Global South markets where weak competition and high demand for connectivity exists (Ho et al., 2023). Nevertheless, Chinese platform internationalization gives substantial power to Chinese firms as they embed third countries within a Chinese 'digital ecosystem' (Hinane El-Kadi, 2024). And the Chinese state plays a proactive role in supporting and securing the international expansion of its digital technology giants, re-emphasizing its commitment to the DSR at the Xi'an World Internet Conference in 2024 (Jiang, 2024). China's top economic planning body, the National Development and Reform Commission, recently published a strategy document pledging to further expand DSR activities as a policy priority in the coming years. As China's platforms develop international commercial expansion strategies which more systematically incorporate the support of state actors and agencies (Oh and No, 2020), they have begun to make significant progress in challenging US dominance of global cyberspace, while assisting Chinese efforts to exercise digital 'infrastructural power' globally (Munn, 2023).

Part II Spheres of Competition

Part I charted the rise of a new system of competition in the global political economy: state platform capitalism. Section 1 provided a schematic history and conceptualization of SPC's logic. Focusing on the world's two foremost digital ecosystems, the United States and China, Sections 2 and 3 pointed out how these differ both in their internal configurations of state-platform relations, and in their mechanisms for international expansion. However, these sections also identified striking similarities between how the Chinese and US states engage with their domestic digital platform firms collaboratively – to ensure their international influence by building geographically extensive 'national' technology stacks.

Discrete, national technology stacks do not, of course, exist in reality. As long as the internet is built upon an open architecture, its total balkanization remains a technical impossibility (Mueller, 2017). Both the United States and Chinese national stacks continue to interpenetrate one another, with considerable Chinese hardware and software used in the United States, and likewise with American technology in China. And both stacks have long since overspilled their national boundaries. The United States in particular exhibits a world-spanning presence, while China is making considerable progress in internationalizing its digital technology ecosystem.

Nevertheless, the emergence of platform giants has made it considerably easier to develop sanitized and nationally centred digital ecosystems, which are difficult, undesirable or inconvenient for users to leave (Kontareva and Kenney, 2023; Mihelj, 2023). The power of first-mover advantage and lock-in, combined with their world-leading capabilities, ties many global users (individuals, firms, and governments) to US digital platforms. And the rise of state capitalist initiatives such as the Clean Network serves to deter adoption of Chinese technology. Where Chinese technologies are in use, bundling practices enabling interoperability between tiered layers of hardware and software make switching to US technologies overly costly and/or burdensome, encouraging further integration with Chinese platforms. As such, while the internet remains immune to 'technical fragmentation', the US and China's national stacks are increasingly 'real abstractions' which shape technology adoption and digital ecosystems well beyond their borders (de Seta, 2021).

In Part II, we elaborate on how these digital ecosystems are increasingly defined by their competition and rivalry, as the United States and China compete to secure platform dominance and to reap the gains of governing through platforms. The United States, as the global digital incumbent, wants to preserve and expand its global platform power by ensuring no rival firms can emerge and that 'latecomer industrial strategies' of the kind pursued by China do not significantly displace US incumbents. The United States is mobilizing an expanding suite of tools to meet this challenge. As a latecomer, China is able to employ a different competition strategy to the United States. It is more accepting of its technologies being integrated with others – including those from the United States – in third countries. Meanwhile the United States has pursued a more rigorous 'stack rationalization' approach, attempting to eliminate as far as possible all traces of Chinese technology it deems threatening. For now, this grants China an advantage, as it can focus more attention on rollout, implementation, and ecosystem development, while the United States must do all this alongside devising exclusionary agreements and encouraging adoption of more expensive alternatives to Chinese suppliers. In the process, SPC competition increasingly and systematically blurs the boundaries between state and private actors.

In the remainder of this text, we examine how this competition unfolds across four different spheres: digital currencies, cybersecurity, standards, and smart cities. We focus on these four spheres because while none are traditional sectors of the economy, but they represent key areas where powerful platform firms and states can reshape rules, institutions, and norms in ways which embed their technologies ever more deeply in third countries' technology stacks.

5 Digital Currencies

The United States is the world's supreme monetary power. The US dollar remains the most widely used currency for cross-border payments by far, representing about half of all trade settlements and 62% of global forex reserves. The dollar maintains an enduring power vis-à-vis its major rivals, including the renminbi (RMB).

> [T]here appears to be just one true pole in the system–namely, the US dollar. The euro, number two globally, lags well behind the greenback; other secondary currencies appear to be little more than niche players; and the RMB is so far back in the race that it still barely even registers. (Benney and Cohen, 2022, 458)

The dollar's dominance is tied up with the outsized role of the US financial system – the world's most powerful by virtually any metric (see Fichtner, 2017). The dollar, the US banking system, and the Fed provide the financial and technical architecture which enable other parties in the world economy to pursue international trade and investment. The global dollar system can itself be understood as a kind of platform, since most greenback transactions do not involve paper currency but rather movements on digital ledgers controlled by messaging infrastructure. Just one-tenth of dollars exists in physical form (Black, 2020). A majority of all dollar deposits are held outside of the United States as 'eurodollars'.

Some economies such as El Salvador are fully dollarized, while a sizeable minority peg their currencies to its value. The US government exerts power over this system through the Federal Reserve's autonomy over broad money creation and the setting of interest rates. Dollar dominance is upheld by the 'swap lines' through which the US Federal Reserve trades dollars for other currencies with central banks' (Pape, 2022), acting as an effective lender of last resort during periods of currency pressure. The dollar's stability, ubiquity, and the liquidity of currency and US financial markets grant the United States the 'exorbitant privilege' of an ability to run endless deficits, alongside the 'exorbitant burden' of consuming (via debt and security issuance) the world's surpluses (Pettis, 2011).

The dollar's global role as financial lubricant within the international banking system is underpinned by the messaging system provided by the Society for Worldwide Interbank Financial Telecommunication (SWIFT), Clearing House Interbank Payments System (CHIPS) which nets and clears interbank payments, and the Fedwire Funds Service which manages central bank transactions. All three are dependent upon American regulatory institutions to function (Carter, 2012). Even SWIFT, despite being formally headquartered in Brussels and regulated by the Belgian central bank, is vulnerable to US financial sanctions due to its Virginia-based mirroring data centre. This has made it a key source of information for US counter-terror operations (Farrell and Newman,

2023). These formal and customary institutions underpin and reinforce dollar dominance and provide the United States with instruments to target and isolate geopolitical rivals. Even US allies such as the EU are not exempt from the long shadow cast by the US dollar, and they have little choice but to comply with US policy (de Goede, 2021).

For developing countries, the combined threat of vulnerability to dollar outflows, alongside the growing threats from Washington to weaponize the dollar, create strong incentives for targeted countries (including China) to bypass these systems. Countries directly targeted by US sanctions and financial power – including China – are eager to find an alternative to the dollar. Even US allies have expressed frustration with the dollar dominated financial system, because they are subject to 'secondary sanctions'. The Russia-Ukraine war has substantially accelerated efforts to break dollar dominance, since the United States and European Union took exceptional measures to restrict Russia's access to the global financial system, leveraged points of integration (including SWIFT) against it, and froze Russian dollar and euro deposits held by Western central banks.

These factors have given a major impetus to China's efforts to construct an alternative monetary and financial architecture to the dollar (Choyleva, 2022). China's Cross-Border Interbank Payment System (CIPS) – established in 2015 – provides an integrated alternative to the combined functions of SWIFT and CHIPS. It combines messaging services with clearing and settlement functions, largely bypassing the existing US-centric financial system (although the two remain interoperable) (Nölke, 2022). CIPS remains roughly 10% the size of SWIFT and CHIPS, but has grown very rapidly. In addition to promoting use of RMB in its bilateral trading relationships, China has also worked to denominate a growing range of assets (such as its abundant rare metals) and associated financial instruments in RMB (Liu, 2024c). To facilitate such efforts, China has built up RMB swap lines with over forty foreign central banks and made $500 bn worth of RMB available to partners (McDowell, 2019; Steil et al., 2024). The RMB's share of all trade financing remains at 7% of world total. However, the share of China's own cross-border payments and receipts denominated in RMB hit a new peak of 53% in 2024, with its use of the dollar to settle trades falling to just 43%. Not surprisingly, the RMB is used amongst China's major trading partners to a considerable degree more than other countries. This has led the IMF to warn of 'geoeconomic fragmentation' into currency blocs (Gopinath, 2024).

China's efforts to build an alternative to the US dollar system are interdependent with the digitalization and platformization of money. Digital tokens are increasingly issued by large platforms and circulate as forms of money. They offer real-time clearing capabilities, while their creators may gain unprecedented transaction-level data. Here, China has a strong first-mover advantage. Its principle private digital currencies (operated by Alibaba Pay and Tencent's WeChat) already accounted for around $7 trillion of transactions in 2022. Their payments are cleared by the central bank's Netsunion system, which captures detailed, real-time transaction data. The People's Bank of China has also developed a central bank digital currency (CBDC), made interoperable with existing private digital currencies by political pressure (Kynge and Sun, 2021). For example, QR-code payment systems for e-CNY now function over Alipay. China's public and private digital currencies appear set to become increasingly merged into the future.

Further, a cross-border, real-time and ledger-based payments system, mBridge, is being developed in tandem with the Bank for International Settlements, the Hong Kong monetary authority, and the Thai, UAE, and Saudi central banks (Jones, 2024).[5] Tencent was involved in designing its architecture, and the project successfully settled a $22 m transaction in 2023. mBridge and the e-CNY raise the possibility of a multi-central bank digital currency bypassing US financial infrastructure (Nölke, 2022). Moreover, private systems like Alipay and Wechat Pay's overseas adoption and interoperability with foreign payments systems are boosted by large-scale Chinese tourism and trade invoicing (Chorzempa and Spielberger, 2025). Choyleva (2022) suggests that the transition to an e-CNY could potentially make China more likely to liberalize its capital accounts, because it offers authorities the capacity to monitor real-time data on inflows and outflows in granular fashion. In theory, authorities could pre-empt capital flight, negating the need for broad-based and permanent capital controls.

However, China's closed capital accounts, the shallowness of its financial markets, and its mostly inconvertible currency mean that the e-CNY and its private-sector digital currencies do not appear to be viable candidates for replacing the dollar in the near to medium term (Deng, 2024). Indeed, while they may be used to settle bilateral trade, they are unlikely to be used as a reserve currency, for transactions not involving China, or for asset denomination. Nor would the present role of the United States as consumer of last resort be upset by more widespread adoption of an e-CNY alone (Eichengreen, 2021). The US role as a backstop consumer, alongside its

---

[5] Concern regarding China's role prompted the BIS to withdraw from mBridge in October 2024, but the project continues to expand.

deep and liquid financial markets, creates an 'organic' demand for dollars (Schwartz, 2019).

China's attempts to undermine the hegemony of the US dollar are also hastening US innovation in this area. In response to both Chinese advances and the emergence of Diem (Meta's ultimately failed digital currency), US Treasury Secretary Janet Yellen initiated exploration of a US CBDC. Discussing the mooted FedCoin, the Federal Reserve (2024) states that 'a CBDC would be the safest digital asset available to the general public, with no associated credit or liquidity risk'. Adoption of a CBDC, however, has been temporarily rejected by the second Trump administration, which favours the use of private cryptocurrencies. The United States prefers to mobilize the dollar's existing global role by supporting its fintech platforms, which in turn offer it enormous surveillance power over global transactions. Payment platforms like Paypal and Venmo operate globally, building 'rails' between the dollar system in which they are rooted – where 'real' money flows and clears slowly – and the token-based currencies they issue and front (O'Dwyer, 2023). The spread of US-backed fintech firms vastly enhances its surveillance and sanctioning capabilities. Using the Bank Secrecy Act (1970), the Patriot Act (2001), and the Anti-Money Laundering Act (2020), US regulators – especially its powerful Financial Crimes Enforcement Network (FinCEN) – have virtually unrestricted access to transaction-level data from US platforms. The United States has been highly active in carving out global market access for its fintech firms (Jutel, 2021).

US-China rivalry in platform-based fintech and digital currencies initially had distinct implications for their conventional banking sectors. In the United States, traditional banks have broadly benefited from fintech from the outset, partnering with platforms and tech giants to leverage digital payments and data analytics capabilities without significant displacement of incumbent power. In contrast, China's state-dominated banking sector initially saw fintech giants (such as Ant Financial and Tencent) as threats, as they displaced existing payment infrastructures and lending functions. However, the technology sector crackdown and e-CNY rollout have served to partly reassert state control over financial infrastructure, and made the Chinese state more prepared to back its private digital currency expansion overseas. Thus, fintech rivalry has bolstered US banks through market-driven alliances, while stabilizing yet constraining China's platforms through enforced collaboration and oversight from state banks. While the open global financial system continues to favour the dollar, its dominance may erode as China's digital currency infrastructure grows, offering alternative trade and finance channels that reduce US leverage to punish or exclude rivals.

6 Cybersecurity

Early in November 1971, Captain John McNish of the USS *Halibut* stared at a grainy image on a control room screen. The *Halibut*, a vintage nuclear-powered submarine from the early 1950s, was anchored at a depth of 120 metres in the Sea of Okhostk off the Kamchatka peninsula – deep inside Soviet territorial waters. McNish watched anxiously via video link as saturation divers, wearing liquid-heated suits, left the submarine's decompression chamber and entered the murky depths. Moving slowly, they used airguns to blow accumulated silt off a bump in the ocean floor, revealing a thick telephone cable that connected the peninsula's naval base to the Russian mainland, and carried unencrypted conversations between senior commanders. After the dust settled, they spent hours fixing a large battery-powered recording device to the cable, before gathering a sample of the voices it transmitted. The *Halibut* would return to Okhostk every six months for the next nine years, gathering and replacing tapes and devices, and returning a treasure trove of strategic intelligence to the Pentagon's analysts in Washington DC (Sontag et al., 1998).

Operation Ivy Bells was one of the Cold War's most elaborate and significant espionage missions. US analysts credit the intelligence it provided with laying the basis for the 1979 SALT II nuclear arms agreement. Today, US agencies continue to tap undersea cables. In 2005, it was revealed that the USS *Jimmy Carter* had cable splicing capabilities which were used to intercept undersea fibre optic networks (Weichert, 2024) – cables which extend over 1 million kilometres and are estimated to carry 99% of all global internet traffic. The US Navy's ongoing efforts to purchase a replacement Virginia-class nuclear attack submarine for the *Carter*, modified for spy usage and including cable tapping and cutting capabilities, signal their ongoing significance (Honrada, 2023).

However, such efforts form only a small part of the National Security Agency's (NSA) arsenal. Far more common is the collection of data from fibre-optic cables' landing stations (as captured in Trevor Paglen's photography).[6] Typically conducted with the consent of cables' operators, devices are placed onto the transition points where undersea cables connect with terrestrial infrastructure networks, refracting the light travelling through them and beaming the mirrored data to US intelligence operatives (Khazan, 2013). Edward Snowden's 2013 leaks revealed the mass data gathering provided by so-called 'upstream' collection programs FAIRVIEW, STORMBREW, BLARNEY, and OAKSTAR, which developed these techniques (see Figure 2). The NSA was able to undertake such expansive surveillance initiatives thanks to the 'extreme willingness'

---

[6] See Sohn (2015). For detail on the vital role of British intelligence services in the NSA's global data gathering operations, see Mainwaring (2020).

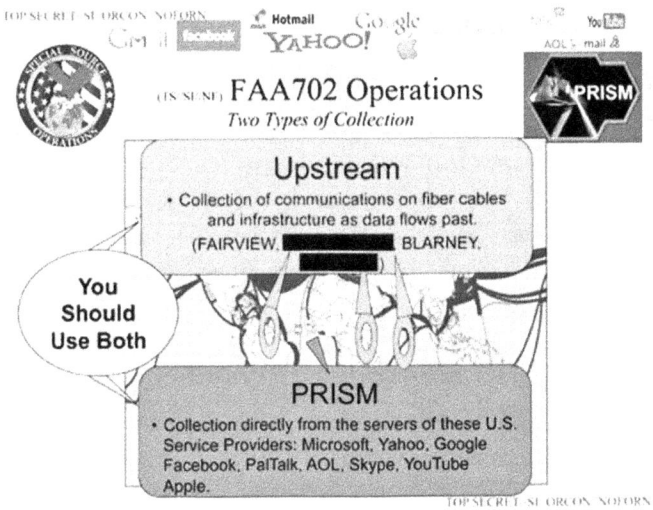

Figure 2 NSA's upstream and downstream data collection
Source: Wikimedia (2013)

of its corporate partners to assist with data collection (Angwin et al., 2015). And unlike wiretaps like Ivy Bells, today's security services can gather far more than simply voice communications.

Undersea fibre-optic internet cables have become a major site of platform investment. Until 2010, legacy telecoms firms like AT&T and Verizon accounted for most investment in subsea cables. But platforms like Meta, Google, and Amazon have driven a $20 bn investment boom in this infrastructure over the past decade. Between 2020 and 2023, Meta, Microsoft, Amazon, and Google accounted for approximately 90% of capital expenditure on new transatlantic cables and 70% of that for transpacific cables (Hamilton and Quinlan, 2024, 98). Platform giants today are also the biggest users of subsea bandwidth by far, accounting for nearly three quarters of all traffic (Salgado, 2023). As such, US firms (both platforms and telcos) own (fully or in part) more than 90 cables, and represent the dominant investors in future projects (Dufetre, 2023).

Much of this new cabling infrastructure transmits platforms' internal data transfer needs (unlike that provided by the telcos operators, which lease capacity to external users). Platforms' exploding investments in physical infrastructure of the internet are directly related to their efforts to expand digital service offerings such as cloud computing, and cement their dominant competitive position. As Blum and Baraka (2022) write of Google's investments in cabling: 'Once the cable is up and running, Google's network managers can prioritize Google's own data traffic, ensuring the performance and reliability of their cloud services – while using that reliability as the services' key selling point.' To lay infrastructure, platforms typically form consortiums with key cable suppliers such as SubCom (US), ASN (France), and NEC (Japan), who produce and lay physical cabling, and telcos like AT&T which provide expertise in deployment, maintenance, and operations.

Internet cables represent an important source of intelligence for those who have access to their data. However, securing them is a monumental task because new market entrants are emerging to meet spiralling demand. While dominated by US platforms, telcos and cabling firms, Chinese operators have also recently become important players in the subsea cabling market. HMN – a spinoff of Huawei now owned by Hengtong (a Chinese private-sector national champion) – is now the world's fourth largest cable supplier. Moreover, China's telcos like China Telecom and China Unicom have become major players in international cable consortia. China's firms privilege cable projects in the Asia Pacific and Eurasia. Alongside their direct commercial objectives, these cable projects can be understood as boosts to China's Digital Silk Road strategy for expanding the activities of its platform giants (Pitron, 2023).

The NSA's experience with tapping landing stations and co-opting cable providers drives concern that China could use similar mechanisms the more it cements its role as a global connectivity provider (Brock, 2023). The United States has sought to contain China's control over internet infrastructure in a number of ways, including inhibiting its firms from investing in projects which interconnect with China. In 2021, for example, the US FCC withdrew permission for Google and Meta to activate the Pacific Light cable – which ran between LA and East Asia – due to its passage through Hong Kong (FitzGerald and Purnell, 2021).

US pressure has also been extended internationally. The SeaMeWe-6 cable, currently under construction, will connect Singapore and France via nine other countries. The international consortium that planned to lay the cable initially involved Chinese firms including HMN. The project was disrupted in 2023 when the United States sanctioned HMN and successfully pushed for SubCom to replace HMN as a supplier. This drove Chinese telcos out of the consortium, and they subsequently announced their own project, EMA (Europe-Middle East-Asia). EMA is a $500 m project that will connect Hong Kong and Hainan with Singapore, Pakistan, Saudi Arabia, Egypt, and France, and thereby undermine US efforts to isolate Hong Kong from the global internet (Brock, 2023). However, currently no new subsea cables are planned to connect either mainland China or Hong Kong internationally beyond 2025. This demonstrates the effectiveness of the US campaign to limit China's connectivity (Takeda and Ban, 2024).

In addition to the upstream cable-tapping programs revealed by Snowden was the downstream 'PRISM' program – mass data-gathering conducted directly from platform companies' servers with their full cooperation. Because platform firms remain domiciled within the United States, they are effectively defenceless against such state claims upon their data. Section 702 of the Foreign Intelligence Services Act (FISA) provides legal pretext and a framework for the NSA to gather communications data from foreign citizens and (to a more limited degree) access US citizens' data. Recent reports show that Section 702 is in widespread use for gathering US citizen data (Ackerman, 2023). It was also recently reported that another key plank of the PRISM program, XKeyscore, 'continues to operate with no judicial and limited congressional oversight despite its potential to capture Americans' communications' (Nakashima, 2021). XKeyscore gathers data on individuals' emails, social media activity, and browsing history from internet service providers and platforms to build detailed user profiles searchable by intelligence analysts. The US CLOUD Act of 2018 permits state access to any US-domiciled cloud provider's overseas data servers (if not contested in court). Since over 70% of global data flows through Loudon, Virginia, due to the intensive clustering of data centres in the city, such provisions are rarely required. Executive Order 12,333 – a piece of Cold War legislation subsequently updated by George W. Bush – offers another legal avenue for surveillance activities to be conducted outside of the FISA framework and rulebook.

The data collected by platforms is increasingly recognized as a geopolitical asset (Gu, 2023). Concerns about election interference, data leaks, industrial espionage, and cyberattacks have fostered moves towards the 'securitization of everything' by governments (Newlove-Eriksson, 2022). The US government's strategy to enhance cybersecurity contributes to the deepened incorporation of American platform firms into the military-industrial complex. Historically, the US government understood cyber threats as 'technical problems to be solved primarily with a combination of defensive and limited deterrence measures' (Alperovitch, 2022, 46). But cybersecurity is increasingly becoming an active field of geopolitical and geoeconomic competition in the face of incidents like the Solarwinds and Volt Typhoon hacks. Donald Trump's first administration responded by making the US Cyber Command a unified combatant command within the US military, and establishing the Cybersecurity and Infrastructure Security Agency (CISA) in the Department of Homeland Security (DHS).

Through the creation of bodies like the DHS's Innovation Programme and its Science and Technology Directorate, Washington has increasingly 'sought to play a market facilitation role with the broader internet technology sector to encourage [state-firm] cooperation' on cybersecurity (Aggarwal and Reddie, 2018, 454). The Department of Defense (2023) *National Security Strategy* established a Bureau of Cyberspace and Digital Policy to boost US platforms' international expansion under the guise of embedding its firms as global cybersecurity providers. When Microsoft purchased a stake in UAE's flagship AI firm G42, on the pretext of securing sensitive data by beating out Chinese investors, the Bureau's Ambassador commented that he had 'been in close contact with UAE Government, with G42, and with Microsoft to help ensure that that investment' (Fick, 2024).

China, meanwhile, has sought to develop a complex assortment of internet management tools and mechanisms to assert control over domestic internet content. These practices enlist platforms as partners and further their commercial ambitions. President Xi formed the Cyberspace Administration of China (CAC) in 2014 to integrate cyber-security policy with the development of the digital economy. The CAC formalized state control over the domestic internet with the National Cyber Security Law of 2016, which formally grants the state substantial legal authority over online content, cross border flows, and jurisdiction over foreign cyber operations inside China (Hong and Goodnight, 2020).

China has moved to restrict usage of US technologies across swathes of the Chinese technology stack by developing greater domestic capabilities. This represents an urgent task given that Creemers (2020, 116) cites Chinese research claiming that in 2014, '82 percent of servers, 73.9 percent of storage equipment, 95.6 percent of operating systems and 91.7 percent of databases' employed in China were provided by foreign, principally US-based, firms (e.g., Microsoft, Cisco, Apple). In an attempt to weaken the position of American technology firms in China, China's SASAC (which oversees its state enterprises) issued Directive 79 in September 2022, directing state firms to remove all foreign software and hardware from their enterprises by 2027 (Lin, 2024). Further, China's stringent data localization requirements have meant significant stores of data have been shifted from foreign servers to Chinese joint-ventures – such as Apple's Chinese user data, formerly hosted in the United States but subsequently moved to Guizhou-Yunshang's servers, a firm backed by the Guizhou provincial government (Kokas, 2018). China's data localization regime appears to have given Chinese platforms an edge when operating in similarly restrictive environments overseas, which pose a greater challenge to US models predicated upon widespread data export (O'Grady, 2024).

A more expansive conception of data and cybersecurity driven by concern about data flows is fuelling concern amongst US policymakers about Chinese platforms' commercial expansion. While the case of Huawei is well known (Liu, 2021), more recently controversies have surrounded digital platforms such as Bytedance's TikTok, the fast-fashion platform Shein, and the e-commerce app Temu – all of which have penetrated global markets to significant degrees. Despite finding no evidence of 'backdoors' being designed into such digital technologies by the Chinese state for surveillance purposes (Gray, 2021), policymakers have aimed to curtail the influence of such platforms by raising security concerns. For example, US lawmakers cast aspersions on TikTok's parent company ByteDance for potentially sharing US user data with the Chinese state (Bartz and Dang, 2021). And the chair of the UK Parliament's Foreign Affairs Committee, Tom Tugendhat (2021), warned of Shein's recommendation algorithms as a 'sinister cross between surveillance and capitalism . . . [deploying] a data collection network to rival many of the world's intelligence agencies'. Temu's advertisements during the 2024 Superbowl drew condemnation from US lawmakers, with Republican Senator Tom Cotton posting on X that Temu 'must allow the Communist Party unfettered access to its data'.[7] Such hyperbolic logic is intelligible if 'cybersecurity' is interpreted to mean control by the United States and its allies over critical stack infrastructures into the future, which growing Chinese commercial prowess is beginning to erode (Tang, 2020).

The United States had long favoured a laissez-faire approach to data flows, supporting stringent restrictions on data localization and privacy requirements, to the benefit of its world-spanning platform firms. But Katherine Tai, then US Trade Representative (USTR), formally reversed the US position on digital trade at the WTO in September 2023 in favour of a more restrictive approach to data flows. Domestically, this was understood as a pitch battle between the 'anti-monopolist' Tai and the National Security Council, which favoured upholding free digital trade (and the predominant position of US platform giants) at all costs. However, the shift in the USTR position signals that the United States is responding to the growing success of Chinese platforms' internationalization by adapting its own data regime and understanding of cyber-security in ways enable states to raise protections against Chinese data exports. Domestically, the Biden administration passed Executive Order 13873 and the Protecting Americans' Data from Foreign Adversaries Act of 2024, both of which set up a framework for limiting bulk data flows to a list of 'adversary' countries (including China). Trump's second administration has upheld these restrictions. Internationally, as Ruiz and Savona (2023) argue, creating 'regulatory space within digital trade could mean precisely setting up parameters on how data flows may be protected from undue interference' – assisting the United States in rebuffing Chinese platforms' advances (particularly in the field of AI) through stricter regulations on data exports. For both the United States and China, then, the goals of advancing platform prowess and state power are converging on an expanded notion of cybersecurity.

---

[7] https://x.com/SenTomCotton/status/1757055483217604697?lang=en.

7 Standards

The setting of global standards may seem like an arcane field. But when it comes to standards for frontier technology, it is also a field of intense geopolitical rivalry that entangles firms as well as governments. A recent White House (2023, 3) strategy document starkly sets out the significance of standards setting for the United States:

> Strength in standards development has been instrumental to the United States' global technological leadership ... Today, however, the United States faces challenges to its longstanding standards leadership, and to the core principles of international standard-setting that, together with likeminded partners, we have upheld for decades. Strategic competitors are actively seeking to influence international standards development, particularly for [critical emerging technologies], to advance their military-industrial policies and autocratic objectives.

Technical standards are of unique significance in platform competition, because standards underpin the compatibility and integration of hardware, software, and services across layers of the technology stack (Bergsen et al., 2022). Control of standards consequently allows platform firms to orchestrate greater control over market structures and industrial ecosystems, enhancing their infrastructural power.

The United States has been able to define the standards that govern the internet and make its transnational expansion possible. Its power over internet standards got off to an inauspicious start. Vint Cerf and Bob Kahn, a young Stanford professor and an ARPA engineer who had worked on aspects of the ARPANET, locked themselves in a hotel conference room in the summer of 1973 and wrote the protocols for TCP/IP – the packet switching rules which continue to enable networking to this day (Levine, 2018). Initially designed for military purposes, Cerf, Kahn and ARPA's success in interconnecting networks eventually spawned the civilian internet. As its creation began to take off, ARPA established the Internet Engineering Task Force (IETF), a private body of sixteen researchers and engineers, to oversee and codify its burgeoning suite of technical standards for networking devices. As Yates and Murphy (2022, 10) write:

> IETF's process differed significantly from that of other private standards bodies; it had no membership (anyone could attend any meeting), no formal/voting, no required balance of stakeholders, no system for representing different parts of the world, and a famously raucous, argumentative style.

Today, the IETF remains the single most important standards-setting body ensuring interoperability in internet governance. But despite its reputation as an 'open' and meritocratic organization, US platform giants increasingly dominate proceedings: '[M]ost IETF participants are from large corporations and key proposals are concentrated into a small group of companies which sponsor individuals' participation in the form of time and travel to annual meetings' (Harcourt et al., 2020, 38). Other important bodies covering internet technology standards include industry-led fora like the W3C, 3GPP, and the IEEE, alongside intergovernmental bodies like the ISO/IEC and the ITU. A recent Atlantic Council study demonstrates that the United States retains overwhelming dominance across these various standards developing organizations (SDOs) (Neaher et al., 2021). And despite their reputation as industry-led and multistakeholder fora, US state agencies have long worked to ensure that US platform firms enjoy influence within SDOs. SDOs function as an important source of international political economic power as they create a smooth global playing field for US tech giants and encode their innovations as the standards upon which in global technology stacks operate (Hill, 2014; Powers and Jablonski, 2015).

Alongside their dominance in international standards stetting bodies, US platforms also dominate private, de facto standard setting (Giblin and Doctorow, 2022). A core component of the platform business model is to anchor de facto standards (such as operating systems or app stores) within technology stacks (Müller et al., 2011). For instance, feature phone internet access across much of the African continent is dominated by Facebook's Free Basics internet service (banned by India, however, on the grounds of its violation of net neutrality). And Google, through its Google Station program, has embedded itself in technology stacks throughout the Global South by rolling out free Wi-Fi at over 5000 locations worldwide (Oyedemi, 2021). Similarly, the AI chip designer NVIDIA designed its platform and code library to only interoperate with its GPU semiconductors, making access indispensable for cutting-edge AI applications (including in China, which is striving to develop a fully autonomous AI industry) (Cusumano, 2023). Such approaches accord with Hart and Kim's (2002, 1) definition of Wintelism as 'strategies for controlling architectural standards in a horizontally segmented industry'.

China is often accused of trying to develop a 'splinternet' by undermining the mixture of standards and protocols that underpin the open internet (Kenyon, 2021). Huawei's development of a 'new IP' (a centralized and de-anonymized alternative to TCP/IP, so far rejected at various SDOs) is a prominent example mobilized by critics (Campanella and Haigh, 2023). But the example is often used misleadingly. China is indeed developing an increasingly comprehensive strategy to counter US state-platform power by challenging its chokehold over internet standardization. But rather than trying to fragment this fundamental architecture (Nanni, 2021), China's strategy is to achieve commercial dominance by becoming a global standards-setting power through technological innovation (Yoo and Mueller, 2024). If successful, its platforms will construct powerful international ecosystems of their own without the need to instantiate 'walled gardens' at the network layer.

China has made concerted attempts to establish formal and informal standards of its own (Murphree and Breznitz, 2018). It successfully developed a domestic standard for 3 G mobile communications (TD-SCDMA), which was accepted as one of three viable standards at the International Telecommunications Union [ITU]) (Gao, 2014). Subsequently, China has developed national-level industrial plans to create international standards since the publication of *Made in China 2025* strategy by the Ministry of Industry and Information Technology (Malkin, 2020). *MiC2025* was followed by the 2018 *China Standards 2035* strategy, which in turn generated the 2022 National Standardization Development Action Plan. The latter aims to set global technological standards in a range of high-technology industries, including explicit targets for software, operating systems and AI development (Wu, 2022). The Chinese state has filled positions at SDOs with political appointees rather than corporate delegates (Rühlig, 2023).

China's concerted efforts have met with some success. China has become amongst the most active members of the International Organization for Standardization (ISO) (Seaman, 2020), while Houlin Zhao served as Secretary-General of the ITU from 2015 to 2022. During the race to develop 5 G technology China successfully achieved 'technical leadership and the first-mover motivation' (Kim et al., 2020, 6), establishing the largest portfolio of standard essential patents (SEPs). Huawei has been the top filer of standard essential patents (SEPs) for 5 G to the standards body 3GPP – ahead of both Ericsson and Qualcomm (Ryugen and Hiroyuki, 2020). One recent investigation estimates Chinese firms (especially Huawei and ZTE) will continue to succeed in the filing of next-generation 5.5 G patents, which will act as milestones on the road to 6 G development. However, US efforts to isolate China appear to have weakened its ability to set 5 G standards vis-à-vis rivals like Cisco and Nokia (Kawakami and Miyajima, 2023).

Beyond this drive into de jure global standard setting, China has also sought to establish de facto standards by encouraging adoption of its technologies. Far from its origins as a messaging service, Tencent's WeChat has become a 'superapp' which encompasses many third-party apps ('mini-apps'). In this way, it has effectively bypassed Android and Apple stores (which suffer restricted access within China) and become a principle interfacing mechanism with the internet for many users (Thun and Sturgeon, 2019). This has enabled Tencent to control a sizeable ecosystem, forcing mini-app developers to conform to its technological standards.

However, setting international standards has proven more challenging, and requires supporting private internet players in their efforts to embed digital technologies in international technology stacks. As noted in Section 3, 'bundling', or full-stack offerings, are a key source of international advantage for China. While its technologies may sometimes be behind the technological frontier, their adoption is nevertheless encouraged either directly by lower costs or by contractual stipulations bundling them with hardware where China is cost-competitive (Seaman, 2020). In this way, the Digital Silk Road serves as a vehicle for setting Chinese technical standards without necessitating their adoption at SDOs. The 20% cost competitiveness in telecommunications hardware offered by Huawei, for instance, incentivizes states to integrate with its networking software ecosystem (Ghiasy and Krishnamurthy, 2020). It also supports adoption of third-party systems, such as China's BDS-3 satellite navigation system, an alternative to US-operated GPS. CITCC recently constructed Tanzania's upgraded broadband network to be compatible only with Huawei routers (Agbebi, 2022, 5). Huawei's HarmonyOS aims to use similar mechanisms to displace Android and Apple, and has so far secured 4% market share in this duopoly (Lan et al., 2022). Inroads into software provision can be more easily made where Chinese internet cabling, data centres, and cloud storage facilities are established (Shen, 2018; Munn, 2020). The rollout of smart city technology, for instance, boosts Chinese software embeddedness across economies and territories more generally (Feldstein, 2020), and allows for the assembly of data from social media and payment apps WeChat and Alipay (Ekman and de Esperanza Picardo, 2020). Similarly, SinoPharm and SinoVac's vaccine provision under the 'health silk road' have bolstered Alibaba's overseas expansion into third countries' digital infrastructures, because they are predicated upon cold-chain storage and delivery of vaccines provided for by Alibaba's cloud-computing system, via the Alibaba Health platform (Habibi and Zhu, 2021).

As de facto standards become adopted, they act as a source of pressure towards aligning 'global technology standards developed by bodies such as the International Telecommunication Union (ITU) with proprietary technologies used by Chinese suppliers' (Robert and Paul, 2020). Aware of how standard-setting capacities have cemented the dominance of its platform giants, US state agencies are increasingly collaborating with big tech firms to limit the space for Chinese (public and private) actors to continue to influence standards. Plantin (2021), for example, cites the case of Open RAN. Nominally a set of standards to ensure interoperability between components in a 5 G network, the Open RAN 'community' mostly consists of US-sponsored SDOs which exclude Chinese players. These groups (such as the Open RAN Policy

Coalition) enjoy backing from the US Federal Communications Commission to work to devise standards enabling the unbundling of 5G hardware and software, in ways which enable US platform giants such as Facebook and Google to collaborate with Huawei rivals Nokia and Ericsson to freeze out Chinese competition.

Similarly, in the AI sphere, Chinese technology firms have become major exporters of AI, as it integrates such services into broader technology and infrastructure deals in areas like health, communications technology, and e-governance. China has successfully captured market share on the African continent by supplying 'cloud storage capabilities, building out data centers, and then integrating all of those technical systems with AI-capable tools' (Bouey et al., 2023, 28). Although smaller than giant US rivals Amazon and Microsoft, Alibaba and Tencent have become major global cloud service providers. They operate large networks of global data centres, which are now being integrated with these platforms' growing AI capabilities such as Alibaba's Qwen (TechNode, 2023; Dobberstein, 2024). China's increasingly competitive position in global AI services provision raises the possibility of its firms being able to set de facto standards in the global industry (Drexel and Kelley, 2023). Domestically, China's regulators have already begun to develop a suite of technical standards for compliance with its increasingly expansive AI and algorithmic regulations (such as techniques for watermarking AI-generated content) (Sheehan, 2024). If these become embedded in its platforms' global offerings, they are likely to become embedded (Rühlig, 2023).

But in AI, as in networking equipment, the United States is using extant standards-setting power as a cudgel with which to weaken China's competitive threat. As *Bloomberg* recently reported, '[s]ome American lawmakers have argued that the United States should play a leading role in the shaping of global AI governance, pointing to China's advancements in the field as a safety and competition concern' (Saraiva, 2024). To this end, the United States recently established an Artificial Intelligence Safety Institute (AISI) within its National Institute of Standards and Technology. The AISI launched a state-industry consortium for AI safety in February 2024, packed with over 200 industry representatives including Google, Meta, Amazon, NVIDIA, and others (Shepardson, 2024). The consortium will help the AISI fulfil its strategy, shared in outline form in May 2024, to 'ensure that AISI's impact is sustained, domestically and internationally, through the adoption of AI safety norms' and standards (Artificial Intelligence Safety Institute, 2024). As it collaborates with its domestic platform giants to produce technical standards for the AI industry, the US government is also driving international initiatives designed to cement its status as a leader of AI standards. It has played a leading role in the

G7 Hiroshima Process for developing international AI standards, which notably excludes China (Habuka and Osa, 2024). At the same time, it recently drove the adoption of the UN's first resolution on AI governance, which calls for international standards for AI interoperability.

To the extent that the United States intervenes to restrict China's ability to standardize its technologies through formal bodies and mobilizes connections between US state institutions and platform giants to head off Chinese competition, Chinese firms and state agencies would seem all the more likely to double down on whatever de facto standardization avenues remain open. This implies a potential for greater fragmentation of global standards, and bodies such as the BRI's Standards Organisation – yet to get off the ground – may be mobilized more actively. This would mean that China establishes a series of de facto standards, while the United States remains able to set de jure standards. If this happens, which set of standards will be more widely used, how they will interact with one another and what the impact will be for the internet as a whole will become ever more intensely contested fields.

8 Smart Cities

The mutually reinforcing trends that have propelled SPC – state capitalism and the platformization of ever grater spheres of economy and society – have also shaped contemporary urbanization. UN Habitat, the supranational body's division that is focused on cities, finalized the New Urban Agenda (NUA) in 2016 after an extensive consultation process with UN member states and civil society stakeholders.[8] By ratifying the NUA, national governments began to reassert authority over urban policy that they had significantly relinquished during neoliberal reforms. Most importantly, the NUA obliges national governments to establish a national urban policy, whose implementation is delegated to local authorities. In other words, national governments are to make urban policies and city governments are to enact them.

National urban policies increasingly leverage technology in pursuit of sustainable urban development. Indeed, the NUA committed states to the rollout of smart city programmes. Smart cities employ information and communication technologies to gather data about the circulation of people and things within cities. Various types of sensors are typically used to collect information, which is acted upon, sometimes in real time, by automated systems. For example, traffic lights can adjust to alleviate gridlock and clear the way for emergency vehicles. Alternatively, people may monitor incoming data in control centres,

---

[8] The UN General Assembly ratified the New Urban Agenda in December, 2016. The full text of the agenda can be found here: https://habitat3.org/the-new-urban-agenda/.

and they are alerted to anomalies by smart city systems. They can review security camera footage and dispatch emergency services if necessary.

Smart cities are paradigmatic examples of platforms insofar as they combine software and hardware in order to intermediate and influence interactions. Some are out-of-the box greenfield projects that are conceived as 'whole system' smart cities from the outset (Gaffney and Robertson, 2018). But greenfield smart cities are few in number, and most smart city technology is incorporated into the urban environment incrementally (Shelton et al., 2015). For example, a city may experiment with an automated traffic control system, while other systems remain decidedly analogue.

Smart city systems make universal assumptions about how cities function, but these are often at odds with particular characteristics of actual urban environments. This explains why smart city systems have oftentimes performed disappointingly, exposing a jarring disjuncture with the techno-utopian ideals celebrated by their corporate proponents (Irazábal and Jirón, 2021). Corporations tried to address this problem by establishing a series of universal standards for smart cities.[9] This effort was taken up by the International Standards Organization, which disseminates standards to national standards agencies. It introduced a series of standards surrounding the representation of urban data, quality management processes and urban governance (Schindler and Marvin, 2018). The idea was to render complex social worlds into a myriad of legible relations among people and things, that could be observed, classified, and ultimately influenced. Proponents of smart city standards hoped that this would enhance the interoperability and effectiveness of smart city technology – if cities could be reduced to a series of relations, then smart city systems could be deployed in heterogeneous urban environments.

Efforts to establish smart city standards began in the early 2010s, when states were reasserting their regulatory authority and platform firms were scaling up their operations at breakneck speed. However, geopolitical rivalry between United States and China was yet to burst into the open. Rather than a competitor in the global smart city market or a geopolitical rival, China's rapidly growing cities were seen as a potentially lucrative market by vendors – with one 2013 stock-take of smart cities asserting that they 'will become the first new industry of the twenty-first century' (Townsend, 2013, 30). Indeed, China was then undergoing an urban revolution unprecedented in human history, and while Beijing made large-scale investments in urban infrastructure in response to the financial crisis, municipal governments in China were responsible for meeting growth targets (Hsing, 2010). Many municipal governments eagerly embraced

---

[9] ISO 37120, 37101, and 30182.

smart city systems, while corporations from the OECD went to great lengths to secure a first-mover advantage in China. For example, South Korea's Samsung coordinated the construction of a greenfield city – Songdo – which served as a 'test bed' for technologies that purportedly presaged the future of 'the new China' (Townsend, 2013).

But selling smart city solutions in China came with a catch – corporations would have to be complicit in the state's large-scale surveillance efforts. American firm Cisco apparently didn't mind. Its software was on display in Songdo, and subsequently packaged in the innocuous sounding 'Peaceful Chongqing' initiative. The *Wall Street Journal* reported in 2011:

> The system, being built in the city of Chongqing over the next two to three years, is among the largest and most sophisticated video-surveillance projects of its kind in China, and perhaps the world. Dubbed 'Peaceful Chongqing,' it is planned to cover a half-million intersections, neighborhoods and parks over nearly 400 square miles, an area more than 25% larger than New York City. (Chao and Clark, 2011)

Cisco supplied the software for Peaceful Chongqing, but like most smart cities, the system involved a number of firms. For example, Chinese firm Hikvision supplied many of the surveillance cameras. In the following decade Hikvision significantly expanded its operations, and it now offers comprehensive security systems that include hardware and software to firms and governments in more than 150 countries (Hikvision, 2024). Hikvision is not alone, as many Chinese firms have participated in roughly 700 smart city initiatives across the country (Yue et al., 2024).

Many of these Chinese 'hidden champions' have become global competitors of their erstwhile American, South Korean and Japanese partners. This has provoked a fierce backlash, with critics pointing out that Chinese firms sell surveillance technology such as facial recognition systems that can be used by governments to monitor political opponents and activists (Atha et al., 2020). Emblematic of this coverage was a *New York Times* story that reported on Ecuador's use of Chinese smart city technology (Mozur et al., 2019). It explained that a vast network of cameras fed images back to 16 monitoring centres and the country's 'feared domestic intelligence agency'. The system, known as ECU-911, was designed and installed by a tie-up between Huawei and the state-owned China National Electronics Import & Export Corporation. The story claimed that there were agreements in place to build similar systems in Venezuela, Bolivia, and Angola. Even more alarmist was an assessment of the operations of Chinese smart city firms in Africa, that concluded '[t]he consequences for human rights on the African continent are likely to be dire' (Gravett, 2022).

Scholars have questioned whether smart city systems built by Chinese firms are genuinely more likely to engender authoritarian governance regimes than technology from their competitors based in the OECD. In reality, governments tend to rely on a range of stakeholders to incrementally deliver smart city technologies into built environments. Rather than contract a Chinese firm to build a 'whole-system' smart city, most cities integrate a patchwork of interlocking systems that evolve over time that include software and hardware from numerous firms. Various systems (e.g. traffic monitoring, facial recognition systems, smart energy management) are provided by 'combinations of Chinese, local, and even foreign actors [that] have participated in the initiation, definition of requirements, technological design, implementation, management and operation, and upgrade of the projects' (Facundo Vila Seoane and Morena Álvarez Velasco, 2024, 155). All of these have the potential to support potentially authoritarian ends, regardless of their state of origin.

Chinese firms have principally captured a significant share of the smart cities market because of their competitiveness. Far from engaging in nefarious authoritarian forms of solidarity, Chinese firms are simply responding to demand from clients – some of whom may have authoritarian aspirations (He, 2024; Majerowicz and de Carvalho, 2024). A more serious criticism is Chinese platforms firms is that they can establish monopoly positions that crowd out local tech firms and inhibit learning-by-doing as they become embedded in urban software systems (Hinane El-Kadi, 2024). And in their efforts to rapidly expand, Chinese firms receive significant support from the state. This includes preferential financing and bundling with hard infrastructure provisioning, as well as access to public funding for research and development.

Alibaba's activity in Kuala Lumpur is illustrative of these dynamics. It initially focused on a series of investments in discrete systems, such as cloud computing and digital logistics management. These were integrated under the Electronic World Trade Platform, whose purpose was to facilitate access to markets and value chains for small and medium-sized enterprises. This has subsequently evolved into a comprehensive smart city initiative called City Brain, that Alibaba first pioneered in Hangzhou. It integrates a series of platforms, facilitating customs clearance and logistics, as well as digital traffic management and 'the transplantation of Alibaba's entire range of cloud-based solutions' (Naughton, 2020a). Importantly, Alibaba's City Brain embeds Chinese digital platforms within Malaysian infrastructure, and this, more than the potential for abuse by autocrats, is what worries US strategists.

Platform initiatives toward integration of numerous disparate systems into a single citywide smart city supersystem that includes software, hardware and infrastructure, heightens security risk by expanding the 'attack surface' open to hostile agents. A report jointly issued by cybersecurity services of the United States, Canada, the UK, Australia, and New Zealand explains:

> This expanded attack surface increases the opportunity for threat actors to exploit a vulnerability for initial access, move laterally across networks, and cause cascading, cross-sector disruptions of infrastructure operations, or otherwise threaten confidentiality, integrity, and availability of organizational data, systems, and networks. (Cybersecurity and Infrastructure Security Agency, 2023, 4)

In the context of this expanded 'attack surface', US-aligned policymakers often argue that the inclusion of Chinese smart city technology offers a 'back door' to critical infrastructure systems. Consequently, the US-China Economic and Security Review Commission commissioned research on Chinese smart cities, and the resultant report recommended that the United States 'should undertake measures to insulate certain types of critical smart infrastructure from supply chain infiltration by Chinese companies, especially core telecommunications infrastructure, electrical power grid systems, and other categories that together make up the foundation of smart city development' (Atha et al., 2020). Doing so would require the creation of multilateral financing vehicles involving US policy banks and allies like Japan and Korea. Even before this report was published, the US-ASEAN Smart Cities Partnership had been announced,[10] and some of its initiatives are indeed funded by the Development Finance Corporation (DFC).[11] The partnership is not limiting its support to countries in ASEAN – for example, it recently supported a small project in Rio de Janeiro.[12] But this is one of many projects in a crowded field – Brazilian cities incorporate smart city technology from firms in the United States, China and many other countries (Majerowicz and de Carvalho, 2024). This mirrors developments elsewhere. Indeed, with few exceptions, most cities will incrementally adopt smart city technology rather than embrace whole-system solutions. To this end, they will combine US and Chinese technology, and in this context American and Chinese firms will jockey for position. For both the Washington and Beijing, smart cities will remain a focal point of competition as they compete to control the integration of digital systems with infrastructure networks.

---

[10] www.usascp.org/.
[11] www.dfc.gov/media/press-releases/dfc-approves-1-billion-investments-global-development.
[12] www.dfc.gov/investment-story/reducing-emissions-introducing-smart-city-infrastructure-brazil.

9 Conclusion

We have made the case that the economic crises of 2008 and 2020 gave rise to two powerful new socio-economic phenomena: *state capitalism* and *platform capitalism*. The new state capitalism, forged in response to disillusionment with neoliberalism in the context of the global economic crisis, has seen states bolster or revive older mechanisms of intervention like state-owned enterprises and subsidies. Meanwhile, they have experimented with newer techniques such as taking golden shares in private firms and pursuing 'market-conforming' industrial policies. These have worked well for individual states in the short run, offering the possibility of a rupture with neoliberal orthodoxy. But their cumulative and long-run impacts appear more concerning – not least because their beggar-thy-neighbour economics and spiralling definitions of 'national security' generate mounting and increasingly disruptive geopolitical tensions.

At the same time, the business sector has been transformed by the success of a small number of giant firms pursuing *platform capitalist* business strategies. Rather than trying to compete in particular product lines, these firms intermediate transactions at scale by enclosing the circulation of capital and exchanges within their proprietary digital ecosystems. Within their platforms, they design and control the protocols governing interactions among users. As such, they have become increasingly infrastructure-like, as businesses and societies are increasingly dependent upon their privately owned digital ecosystems. Platforms, moreover, are highly spatially concentrated – with the large majority based in a handful of cities in either the United States or China.

Each trend has separately received considerable scholarly attention and analysis, but few have stopped to ask exactly how the resurgence of states as powerful and interventionist economic actors relates to the rise of giant, technologically sophisticated digital platform firms whose operations span national boundaries and concentrate power in private hands. Although states and platform firms' interests do sometimes diverge, our core contention is that their relationships are increasingly close and their interests symbiotic. While platform firms carefully cultivate a 'Californian ideology' of opposition to state power, in fact, they have – in the United States and China alike – sought and received extensive state protection and support, especially in their international operations. States have provided steady and reliable custom for platform giants, especially for military and national security purposes, while offering considerable support to their overseas operations. Meanwhile, platforms have embraced connections with states eager to project power internationally – an aim for which platforms are the ideal vehicle, due to their vast scale, governance capacities, and their emerging role as owners and operators of critical digital infrastructure.

We have provided considerable evidence for how states and platforms have become intertwined in the practice of state platform capitalism. The nature of digital platforms means that competition is not being fought out in traditional markets for product lines, as in, for instance, US competition in the auto industry with Japan and West Germany in the post-war period. Instead, platforms span multiple product lines and offerings, as they build out private ecosystems. We have shown on how state platform capitalist competition unfolds beyond the sphere of traditionally-defined markets – encompassing contestation over digital currencies, cybersecurity, standards-setting, and over smart city technologies. In these spheres, as in others not discussed here, US and Chinese states collaborate extensively with their respective platform giants to secure advantage and to embed their technologies within third countries' technology stacks into the future.

How state platform capitalist competition will continue to unfold remains unclear. The ongoing 'digitalization of everything' is likely to concentrate ever more power in the hands of giant platform firms. This clearly contains risks – not least that spiralling paranoia about the 'weaponisation of everything' (Galeotti, 2022) leads states towards vastly expensive programs to try to wrest control over digital nodes and networks from potential rivals. Moreover, while the internet itself remains unlikely to fragment completely, state-platform capitalist competition is undoubtedly driving a growing disintegration of digital technology ecosystems. Efforts such as the 'Clean Network' – while itself formally abandoned – are only likely to deepen as the United States strives to contain China's emerging digital prowess. Similarly, while patchwork and hybrid technology stacks will likely persist, Chinese efforts towards global digital expansion will also undoubtedly serve to concentrate technology power in the hands of its platform giants, especially across the Global South. This uneasy global layering of rival and geographically extensive platform technologies will surely continue to be a source of tension and conflict into the future.

The geopoliticization of digital platform technologies also obscures the inherent challenges they pose to contemporary societies. At present, platform firms' operational logics are driven by their own profit and growth motives, increasingly infused with the geopolitical goals of states. This does not leave much room for alternative visions of digital power attuned to meeting social goals. Would a TikTok wrested from its Chinese parent company and handed to a US billionaire be any more socially responsible than it is presently? Exerting popular and democratic control over digital platform technologies surely means rejecting states' drives to enlist them into the Second Cold War. It also requires conceiving them as critical social infrastructures which should be secure, transparent, and operated in the public interest (Van Dijck, 2020). Judging by the material assembled here, we remain some way from such a vision.

References

Abels, Joscha & Bieling, Hans-Jürgen 2024. 'The geoeconomics of infrastructures: Viewing globalization and global rivalry through a lens of infrastructural competition', *Globalizations*, 21(4): 722–739.

Ackerman, Spencer. 2023. 'The FBI Is Back to Its Old Habits: Illegally Spying on Protesters'. *The Nation*, 9 June 2023.

Adkins, Lisa, Cooper, Melinda & Konings, Martijn 2020. *The Asset Economy*: Property Ownership and the New Logic of Inequality. Cambridge: Polity Press.

Agbebi, Motolani. 2022. 'Chinas Digital Silk Road and Africa's Technological Future' [Online]. www.cfr.org/sites/default/files/pdf/Chinas%20Digital%20Silk%20Road%20and%20Africas%20Technological%20Future_FINAL.pdf.

Aggarwal, Vinod K & Reddie, Andrew W 2018. 'Comparative industrial policy and cybersecurity: the US case', *Journal of Cyber Policy*, 3(3): 445–466.

Alami, Ilias, DiCarlo, Jessica, Rolf, Steve & Schindler, Seth. 2025. 'The New Frontline: The US-China Battle for Control of Global Networks' [Online]. www.tni.org/en/article/the-new-frontline.

Alami, Ilias & Dixon, Adam D. 2020a. 'State capitalism (s) redux? Theories, tensions, controversies', *Competition & Change*, 24(1): 70–94.

Alami, Ilias & Dixon, Adam D. 2021. 'Uneven and combined state capitalism', *Environment and Planning A: Economy and Space*, 55(1): 72–99.

Alami, Ilias & Dixon, Adam D. 2024. *The Spectre of State Capitalism*. Oxford: Oxford University Press.

Alami, Ilias & Dixon, Adam D. 2020b. 'The strange geographies of the "new" state capitalism', *Political Geography*, 82.

Allen, Matthew M. C., Wood, Geoffrey T. & Keller, Matthew R. 2022. 'State Capitalism: Means and Dimensions', In Wright, Mike, Wood, Geoffrey T., Cuervo-Cazurra, Alvaro et al. (eds.) *Oxford Handbook of State Capitalism and the Firm*. Oxford: Oxford University Press.

Allen-Ebrahimian, Bethany. 2021. 'Former Google CEO and Others Call for U.S.-China Tech "Bifurcation"'. *Axios*, 26 January 2021.

Alperovitch, Dmitri 2022. 'The case for cyber-realism: Geopolitical problems don't have technical solutions', *Foreign Affairs*, 101, 44–51.

America's Frontier Fund. 2022. 'Mission' [Online]. https://americasfrontier.org/mission.

Angwin, Julia, Savage, Charlie, Larson, Jeff et al . 2015. 'AT&T Helped U.S. Spy on Internet on a Vast Scale'. *New York Times*, 15 August 2015.

Arboleda, Martín & Purcell, Thomas F. 2021. 'The turbulent circulation of rent: towards a political economy of property and ownership in supply chain capitalism', *Antipode*, 53(6): 1599–1618.

Artificial Intelligence Safety Institute. 2024. 'The United States Artificial Intelligence Safety Institute: Vision, Mission, and Strategic Goals' [Online]. Washington, DC: NIST/US AISI. www.nist.gov/system/files/documents/2024/05/21/AISI-vision-21May2024.pdf.

Atha, Katherine, Callahan, Jason, Chen, John et al. 2020. *China's Smart Cities Development*: SOS International LLC.

Babić, Milan, Dixon, Adam D. & Liu, Imogen T. 2022. 'Moving Forward: Understanding the Geoeconomic Decade of the 2020s', *The Political Economy of Geoeconomics: Europe in a Changing World*. Springer.

Bakonyi, Jutta & Darwich, May 2024. 'Infrastructures and international relations: A critical reflection on materials and mobilities', *International Studies Review*, 26(4): viae046.

Baltz, Matthew J. 2022. 'What lies beneath the "tariff man"? The Trump administration's response to China's "state capitalism"'. *Contemporary Politics*, 28(3): 328–346.

Bartz, Diane & Dang, Sheila. 2021. 'TikTok Tells U.S. Lawmakers It Does Not Give Information to China's Government'. *Reuters*, 26 October 2021.

Benney, Tabitha M. & Cohen, Benjamin J 2022. 'The international currency system revisited', *Review of Keynesian Economics*, 10(4): 443–461.

Bergsen, Pepijn, Caeiro, Carolina, Moynihan, Harriet, Schneider-Petsinger, Marianne & Wilkinson, Isabella 2022. 'Digital trade and digital technical standards', *Chatham House*. www.chathamhouse.org/2022/01/digital-trade-and-digital-technical-standards.

Black, David B. 2020. 'Who Needs Cryptocurrency FedCoin When We Already Have A National Digital Currency?'. *Forbes*, 1 March 2020.

Bloomberg News. 2023. 'China Widens Lead Over US in AI Patents After Beijing Tech Drive'. *Bloomberg*, 24 October 2023.

Blum, Andrew & Baraka, Carey. 2022. 'Sea change: Google and Meta's new subsea cables mark a tectonic shift in how the internet works, and who controls it', *Rest of World*. https://restofworld.org/2022/google-meta-underwater-cables/.

Bordelon, Brendan & Oprysko, Caitlin. 2023. 'Everybody in Washington Wants a Byte of the CHIPS Law'. *Politico*, 17 March 2023.

Bouey, Jennifer, Hu, Lynn, Scholl, Keller et al. 2023. *China's AI Exports: Technology Distribution and Data Safety*, Santa Monica, CA: RAND Corporation.

Bradford, Anu 2023. *Digital Empires: The Global Battle to Regulate Technology*. Oxford: Oxford University Press.

Bratton, Benjamin H. 2016. *The Stack: On Software and Sovereignty*. Cambridge: MIT Press.

Bratton, Benjamin. H. 2018. 'On hemispherical stacks: Notes on multipolar geopolitics and planetary-scale computation', In Wang Shaoqiang (ed.) *As We May Think: Feedforward: The 6th Guangzhou Triennial*, pp. 77–85.

Bremmer, Ian 2009. 'State capitalism comes of age: The end of the free market?', *Foreign Affairs*, 88(3): 40–55.

Brenner, Robert 2006. *The Economics of Global Turbulence: The Advanced Capitalist Economies from Long Boom to Long Downturn, 1945–2005*. London: Verso.

Brock, Joe. 2023. 'China plans $500 million subsea internet cable to rival US-backed project'. *Reuters*, 6 April 2023.

Brown, Michael. 2021. 'Preparing the U.S. for a Superpower Marathon with China' [Online]. Defense Innovation Unit. https://apps.dtic.mil/sti/pdfs/AD1123770.pdf.

Brynjolfsson, Erik & McAfee, Andrew 2014. *The Second Machine Age: Work, Progress, and Prosperity in a Time of Brilliant Technologies*. WW Norton.

Campanella, Edoardo & Haigh, John. 2023. 'China Wants to Run Your Internet'. *Foreign Policy*, 25 August.

Cao, Ann. 2022. 'Jack Ma-backed Free Trade Hub in Thailand Begins Trial Operation'. *South China Morning Post*, 12 December 2022.

Carter, Barry E. Farha, Ryan M. 2012. 'Overview and Operation of U.S. Financial Sanctions, Including the Example of Iran Symposium Article', *Georgetown Journal of International Law*, 44(3): 903–913.

Cennamo, Carmelo 2021. 'Competing in Digital Markets: A Platform-Based Perspective', *Academy of Management Perspectives*, 35(2): 265–291.

Chan, Ngai Keung & Kwok, Chi 2022. 'The Politics of Platform Power in Surveillance Capitalism: A Comparative Case Study of Ride-Hailing Platforms in China and the United States', *Global Media and China*, 7(2): 131–150.

Chan, Ngai Keung & Kwok, Chi 2024. 'State-led embeddedness: Analyzing the discursive construction of platforms and social good in Beijing, Hangzhou, Shanghai, and Shenzhen', *Global Media and China*, 9(3): 362–383.

Chandler Jr, Alfred D. 1977. *The Visible Hand: The Managerial Revolution in American Business*, Cambridge, MA: Harvard University Press.

Chao, Loretta & Clark, Don. 2011. 'Cisco Poised to Help China Build Surveillance Project'. *Wall Street Journal*, 5 July 2011.

Chen, Fa 2022. 'Variable interest entity structures in China: are legal uncertainties and risks to foreign investors part of China's regulatory policy?', *Asia Pacific Law Review*, 29(1): 1–24.

Cheung, Tai Ming 2022. *Innovate to Dominate: The Rise of the Chinese Techno-Security State*. Ithaca: Cornell University Press.

Chorzempa, Martin & Spielberger, Lukas 2025. 'Significant, but not systemic: The challenge of China's efforts to rival Western financial predominance', *Peterson Institute for International Economics Policy Brief*, 25–24. www.piie.com/sites/default/files/2025-05/pb25-4.pdf.

Choyleva, Diana & Dinny McMahon. 2022. *China's Quest for Self-Reliance: How Beijing Plans to Decouple from the Dollar-Based Global Trading and Financial System* [Online]. www.wilsoncenter.org/publication/chinas-quest-self-reliance-how-beijing-plans-decouple-dollar-based-global-trading-and.

Collier, Andrew 2022. *China's Technology War: Why Beijing Took Down its Tech Giants*. Singapore: Springer.

Comunello, Francesca & Mulargia, Simone 2023. 'Does the "Platform Society" Mean the End of the "Network Society?" Reflections on Platforms and the Structure and Dynamics of Networks', *American Behavioral Scientist*, 67(7): 859–871.

Creemers, Rogier. 2019. *The International and Foreign Policy Impact of China's Artificial Intelligence and Big-Data Strategies* [Online]. Wright, Nicholas D. www.jstor.org/stable/resrep19585.23.

Creemers, Rogier 2020. 'China's conception of cyber sovereignty', In Dennis Broeders & Bibi van den Berg (eds.) *Governing Cyberspace: Behavior, Power and Diplomacy*, 107–145. Lanham: Rowman & Littlefield.

Cusumano, Michael 2023. 'NVIDIA at the Center of the Generative AI Ecosystem–For Now', *Communications of the ACM*, 67(1): 33–35.

Cybersecurity and Infrastructure Security Agency. 2023. 'Cybersecurity Best Practices for Smart Cities' [Online]. www.cisa.gov/resources-tools/resources/cybersecurity-best-practices-smart-cities.

Davis, Gerald F. 2022. *Taming Corporate Power in the 21st Century*. Cambridge University Press.

Davis, Mark & Xiao, Jian 2021. 'De-Westernizing Platform Studies: History and Logics of Chinese and U.S. Platforms', *International Journal of Communication*, 15(2021): 103–122.

de Goede, Marieke 2021. 'Finance/security infrastructures', *Review of International Political Economy*, 28(2): 351–368.

de Seta, Gabriele 2021. 'Gateways, sieves, and domes: On the infrastructural topology of the Chinese stack', *International Journal of Communication*, 15: 2669–2692.

Deng, Harry 2024. 'Negotiating currency internationalization: An infrastructural analysis of the digital RMB', *Finance and Society*, 10(1): 1–17.

Department of Defense. 2023. *2023 'Cyber Strategy'* [Online]. Washington, DC. https://media.defense.gov/2023/Sep/12/2003299076/-1/-1/1/2023_DOD_Cyber_Strategy_Summary.PDF.

Dietz, Miklos, Khan, Hamza & Rab, Istvan. 2020. 'How Do Companies Create Value from Digital Ecosystems' [Online]. www.mckinsey.com/~/media/McKinsey/Business%20Functions/McKinsey%20Digital/Our%20Insights/How%20do%20companies%20create%20value%20from%20digital%20ecosystems/How-do-companies-create-value-from-digital-ecosystems-vF.pdf.

Dobberstein, Laura. 2024. 'Alibaba is taking its cloud to Mexico'. *The Register*, 24 May 2024.

Drexel, Bill & Kelley, Hannah. 2023. 'Behind China's Plans to Build AI for the World'. *Politico*. www.politico.com/news/magazine/2023/11/30/china-global-ai-plans-00129160.

Drezner, Daniel W. 2024. 'How everything became national security: And national security became everything', *Foreign Affairs*, 103(5): 122–135.

Dufetre, Romain 2023. *The Data Roads under the Seas: American Hegemony over the Global Undersea Cable Network and its Potential Challengers*. Master of Arts, Chicago: University of Chicago.

Durand, Cédric 2020. *Technoféodalisme: Critique de l'économie numérique*: Zones.

Eichengreen, Barry 2021. 'The Dollar and its Discontents', *Seoul Journal of Economics*, 34(1): 1–16.

Ekman, Alice & de Esperanza Picardo, Cristina. 2020. 'Towards Urban Decoupling? China's Smart City Ambitions at the Time of Covid-19' [Online]. www.jstor.org/stable/resrep25030.

Facundo Vila Seoane, Maximiliano & Morena Álvarez Velasco, Carla 2024. 'The Chinese surveillance state in Latin America? Evidence from Argentina and Ecuador', *The Information Society*, 40(2): 154–167.

Fannin, Rebecca 2019. *Tech Titans of China: How China's Tech Sector is Challenging the World by Innovating Faster, Working Harder, and Going Global*. Boston: Nicholas Brealey.

Farrell, Henry & Newman, Abraham 2023. *Underground Empire: How America Weaponized the World Economy*. New York: Henry Holt.

Federal Reserve 2024. 'Central Bank Digital Currency (CBDC)' [Online]. www.federalreserve.gov/central-bank-digital-currency.htm.

Feldstein, Steven 2020. 'Testimony before the U.S.-China Economic and Security Review Commission: Hearing on China's Strategic Aims in Africa' [Online]. www.uscc.gov/sites/default/files/Feldstein_Testimony.pdf.

References

Fichtner, Jan 2017. 'Perpetual decline or persistent dominance? Uncovering Anglo-America's true structural power in global finance', *Review of International Studies*, 43(1): 3–28.

Fick, Nathaniel C. 2024. The United States' International Cyberspace and Digital Policy Strategy. United States Department of State.

FitzGerald, Drew & Purnell, Newley. 2021. 'Facebook Drops Plan to Run Fiber Cable to Hong Kong Amid U.S. Pressure'. *Wall Street Journal*, 10 March 2021.

Foster, Christopher & Azmeh, Shamel 2020. 'Latecomer economies and national digital policy: An industrial policy perspective', *The Journal of Development Studies*, 56(7): 1247–1262.

Gaffney, Christopher & Robertson, Cerianne 2018. 'Smarter than Smart: Rio de Janeiro's flawed emergence as a smart city', *Journal of Urban Technology*, 25(3): 47–64.

Galeotti, Mark 2022. *The Weaponisation of Everything by Mark Galeotti*, Princeton: Yale University Press.

Galloway, Alexander R. 2004. *Protocol: How Control Exists After Decentralization*. Cambridge: MIT Press.

Gao, Xudong 2014. 'A latecomer's strategy to promote a technology standard: The case of Datang and TD-SCDMA', *Research Policy*, 43(3): 597–607.

Gawer, Annabelle 2022. 'Digital platforms and ecosystems: Remarks on the dominant organizational forms of the digital age', *Innovation*, 24(1): 110–124.

Gentile, Gian, Shurkin, Michael, Evans, Alexandra T et al. 2021. *A History of the Third Offset, 2014–2018* [Online]. Santa Monica, CA.

Gertz, Geoffrey & Evers, Miles M 2020. 'Geoeconomic competition: Will state capitalism win?', *The Washington Quarterly*, 43(2): 117–136.

Ghiasy, Richard & Krishnamurthy, Rajeshwari 2020. 'The digital silk road–strategic repercussions for the EU and India', *IPCS-LAC DSR Policy Paper*, 16: 1–26.

Ghosh, Indranil. 2025. 'How Trump's Gulf Trip Turned Oil Kingdoms into Tech Superpowers'. *rest of world*, 15 May 2025.

Giblin, Rebecca & Doctorow, Cory 2022. *Chokepoint Capitalism*. Boston: Beacon Press.

González, Roberto J. 2024. 'How Big Tech and Silicon Valley are Transforming the Military-Industrial Complex' [Online]. https://watson.brown.edu/costsofwar/files/cow/imce/papers/2023/2024/Silicon%20Valley%20MIC.pdf.

Gopinath, Gita 2024. 'Speech: Geopolitics and its Impact on Global Trade and the Dollar' [Online]. www.imf.org/en/News/Articles/2024/05/07/sp-geopolitics-impact-global-trade-and-dollar-gita-gopinath.

Grabher, Gernot 2025. 'The disruption delusion: Machines, networks, and the platformization of industrial production', *Sociologica*, 19(1): 125–153.

Gravett, Willem H. 2022. 'Digital neocolonialism: The Chinese surveillance state in Africa', *African Journal of International and Comparative Law*, 30(1): 39–58.

Gray, Joanne 2021. 'The geopolitics of "platforms": the TikTok challenge', *Internet Policy Review*, 10(2). https://doi.org/10.14763/2021.2.1557.

Gregg, Aaron 2021. 'NSA Quietly Awards $10 Billion Cloud Contract to Amazon, Drawing Protest from Microsoft'. *Washington Post*, 11 August 2021.

Grön, Kirsikka, Chen, Zhuo & Ruckenstein, Minna 2023. 'Concerns with infrastructuring: Invisible and invasive forces of digital platforms in Hangzhou, China', *International Journal of Communication*, 1717: 5993–6009.

Gu, Hongfei 2023. 'Data, big tech, and the new concept of sovereignty', *Journal of Chinese Political Science*, 29(4): 1–22.

Gupta, Neeti, Urmetzer, Florian & Ansari, Shahzad 2025. 'Big-tech strategic partnerships in artificial intelligence', *International Journal of Business and Management*, 20(3): 57–72.

Habibi, Nader & Zhu, Hans Yue 2021. 'The Health Silk Road as a New Direction in China's Belt and Road Strategy in Africa' [Online]. https://heller.brandeis.edu/gds/pdfs/working-papers/china-africa-2021.pdf.

Habuka, Hiroki & Osa, David U. Socol de la 2024. *Shaping Global AI Governance: Enhancements and Next Steps for the G7 Hiroshima AI Process* [Online]. www.csis.org/analysis/shaping-global-ai-governance-enhancements-and-next-steps-g7-hiroshima-ai-process.

Hameiri, Shahar & Jones, Lee 2024. 'China, international competition and the stalemate in sovereign debt restructuring: Beyond geopolitics', *International Affairs*, 100(2): 691–710.

Hamilton, Daniel S. & Quinlan, Joseph P. 2024. 'The Transatlantic Economy 2024' [Online]. Washington, DC.

Harcourt, Alison, Christou, George & Simpson, Seamus 2020. *Global Standard Setting in Internet Governance*. Oxford: Oxford University Press.

Hardaker, Sina 2025. 'From bytes to bricks: Advocating for a turn toward platform-led infrastructuralization in economic geography', *Progress in Economic Geography*, 3(1): 100038.

Harris, Peter & Trubowitz, Peter 2021. 'The Politics of Power Projection: The Pivot to Asia, Its Failure, and the Future of American Primacy', *The Chinese Journal of International Politics*, 14(2): 187–217.

Hart, Jeffrey A. & Kim, Sangbae 2002. 'Explaining the resurgence of US competitiveness: The rise of Wintelism', *The Information Society*, 18(1): 1–12.

Harvey, David 1981. 'The spatial fix–Hegel, von Thunen, and Marx', *Antipode*, 13(3): 1–12.

He, Yujia 2024. 'Chinese digital platform companies' expansion in the Belt and Road countries', *The Information Society*, 40(2): 96–119.

Heeks, Richard, Ospina, Angelica V., Foster, Christopher et al. 2024. 'China's digital expansion in the Global South: Systematic literature review and future research agenda', *The Information Society*, 40(2): 69–95.

Hikvision 2024. 'About Hikvision' [Online]. www.hikvision.com/us-en/about-us/hikvision-global/.

Hill, Richard 2014. 'Internet governance: The last gasp of colonialism, or imperialism by other means?', In Radu, Roxana, Chenou, Jean-Marie & Weber, Rolf H. (eds.) *The Evolution of Global Internet Governance: Principles and Policies in the Making*. Berlin, Heidelberg: Springer Berlin Heidelberg.

Hinane El-Kadi, Tin 2024. 'Learning along the Digital Silk Road? Technology transfer, power, and Chinese ICT corporations in North Africa', *The Information Society*, 40(2): 136–153.

Ho, Chun-Yu, Narins, Thomas P. & Sung, Won 2023. 'Developing information and communication technology with the belt and road initiative and the digital silk road', *Telecommunications Policy*, 47(10): 102672.

Hong, Yu & Goodnight, G. Thomas 2020. 'How to think about cyber sovereignty: The case of China', *Chinese Journal of Communication*, 13(1): 8–26.

Honrada, Gabriel. 2023. 'New US spy sub built for seabed war with China – Asia Times'. *Asia Times*, 24 April 2023.

Horowitz, Michael C., Allen, Gregory C., Kania, Elsa B. & Scharre, Paul 2018. *Strategic Competition in an Era of Artificial Intelligence*. Washington D.C.: Center for a New American Security.

Hosseini, Hamidreza 2023. 'Platform Economy 2023: U.S. Leads; Europe Lags' [Online]. www.platformeconomy.io/blog/platform-economy-2023-u-s-leads-europe-lags.

Hsing, You-Tien 2010. *The Great Urban Transformation: Politics of Land and Property in China*: New York: Oxford University Press.

Huang, Jingyang & Tsai, Kellee S. 2022. 'Securing authoritarian capitalism in the digital age: The political economy of surveillance in China', *The China Journal*, 88(1): 2–28.

Huang, Raffaele & Kubota, Yoko 2024. 'Microsoft Asks Hundreds of China-Based AI Staff to Consider Relocating Amid U.S.-China Tensions'. *Wall Street Journal*, 16 March 2024.

Hung, Ho-fung 2022. *Clash of Empires: From 'Chimerica' to the 'New Cold War'*: Cambridge: Cambridge University Press.

Hurun 2022. 'Hurun China 500' [Online]. www.hurun.net/en-US/Rank/HsRankDetails?pagetype=ctop500.

Hurun 2024. 'Global Unicorn Index 2024' [Online]. www.hurun.net/en-US/Info/Detail?num=9K1G2SK5X7CX.

IMF 2020. 'State-Owned Enterprises: the Other Government', *Fiscal Monitor, April 2020*. International Monetary Fund.

IMF 2024. 'Government expenditure, percent of GDP' [Online]. www.imf.org/external/datamapper/exp@FPP.

IQT 2024. 'Innovation on a Mission' [Online]. www.youtube.com/watch?v=RjyXgHMKVdc.

Irazábal, Clara & Jirón, Paola 2021. 'Latin American smart cities: Between worlding infatuation and crawling provincialising', *Urban Studies*, 58(3): 507–534.

Jacobides, Michael G. 2019. 'In the ecosystem economy, what's your strategy?', *Harvard Business Review*, 97(5): 128–137.

Jia, Kai, Kenney, Martin & Zysman, John 2018. 'Global Competitors? Mapping the Internationalization Strategies of Chinese Digital Platform Firms', In van Tulder, Rob, Verbeke, Alain & Piscitello, Lucia (eds.) *International Business in the Information and Digital Age*, pp. 187–215. Bingley: Emerald.

Jia, Lianrui 2021. 'Building China's tech superpower: State, domestic champions and foreign capital', *Power and Authority in Internet Governance*. Routledge.

Jia, Lianrui & Winseck, Dwayne 2018. 'The political economy of Chinese internet companies: Financialization, concentration, and capitalization', *International Communication Gazette*, 80(1): 30–59.

Jiang, Ben 2024. 'Beijing promotes China-led vision for Digital Silk Road at Xian forum'. *South China Morning Post*, 16 April 2024.

Jones, Marc 2024. 'Saudi Arabia joins BIS- and China-led central bank digital currency project'. *Reuters*, 5 June 2024.

Jutel, Olivier 2021. 'Blockchain imperialism in the Pacific', *Big Data & Society*, 8(1): 2053951720985249.

Kania, Elsa B. & Laskai, Lorand 2021. *Myths and Realities of China's Military-Civil Fusion Strategy*. Washington D.C.: Center for a New American Security.

Kawakami, Takashi & Miyajima, Shiho 2023. 'China seeks leg up in 6 G standards race with faster wireless tech'. *Nikkei Asia*.

Kenney, Martin & Zysman, John 2016. 'The rise of the platform economy', *Issues in Science and Technology*, 32(3): 61.

Kenney, Martin & Zysman, John 2019. 'Unicorns, Cheshire cats, and the new dilemmas of entrepreneurial finance', *Venture Capital*, 21(1): 35–50.

Kenney, Martin & Zysman, John 2020. 'The platform economy: Restructuring the space of capitalist accumulation', *Cambridge Journal of Regions, Economy and Society*, 13(1): 55–76.

Kenyon, Flavia 2021. 'China's 'Splinternet' Will Create a State-Controlled Alternative Cyberspace'. *The Guardian*, 3 June 2021.

Khazan, Olga 2013. 'The Creepy, Long-Standing Practice of Undersea Cable Tapping'. *The Atlantic*, 16 July 2013.

Kim, Mi-jin, Lee, Heejin & Kwak, Jooyoung 2020. 'The changing patterns of China's international standardization in ICT under techno-nationalism: A reflection through 5 G standardization', *International Journal of Information Management*, 54, 102–145.

Klinge, Tobias J, Hendrikse, Reijer, Fernandez, Rodrigo & Adriaans, Ilke 2023. 'Augmenting digital monopolies: A corporate financialization perspective on the rise of Big Tech', *Competition & Change*, 27(2): 332–353.

Kokas, Aynne 2018. 'Platform patrol: China, the United States, and the global battle for data security', *The Journal of Asian Studies*, 77(4): 923–933.

Konings, Martijn 2010. 'Neoliberalism and the American state', *Critical Sociology*, 36(5): 741–765.

Konkel, Frank 2020. 'CIA Awards Secret Multibillion-Dollar Cloud Contract' [Online]. www.nextgov.com/it-modernization/2020/11/exclusive-cia-awards-secret-multibillion-dollar-cloud-contract/170227/.

Kontareva, Alina & Kenney, Martin 2023. 'National markets in a world of global platform giants: The persistence of Russian domestic competitors', *Policy & Internet*, 15(3): 327–350.

Kurlantzick, Joshua 2016. *State capitalism: How the return of statism is transforming the world*. Oxford: Oxford University Press.

Kwet, Michael 2019. 'Digital colonialism: US empire and the new imperialism in the Global South', *Race & Class*, 60(4): 3–26.

Kynge, James & Sun, Yu 2021. 'Virtual control: The agenda behind China's new digital currency'. *Financial Times*, 17 February 2021.

Lan, Sai, Chen, Junsong & Liu, Kun 2022. Open Source Software Platform Innovation in China: Past, Present, and the Future. In Serdar S. Durmusoglu (eds.) Chinese Innovation and Branding Leaps, pp. 39–77. Singapore: World Scientific Publishing Co.

Langley, Paul & Leyshon, Andrew 2017. 'Platform capitalism: The intermediation and capitalization of digital economic circulation', *Finance and Society*, 3(1): 11–31.

Larsen, Benjamin 2019. *Drafting China's National AI Team for Governance – DigiChina* [Online]. https://digichina.stanford.edu/work/drafting-chinas-national-ai-team-for-governance/.

Lehdonvirta, Vili 2022. *Cloud Empires: How Digital Platforms are Overtaking the State and How We Can Regain Control*. Cambridge: MIT Press.

Leoni, Zeno 2022. 'The economy-security conundrum in American grand strategy: foreign economic policy toward China from Obama to Biden', *China International Strategy Review*, 4(2): 320–334.

Lessig, Lawrence 2000. 'Code is law', *Harvard Magazine*. https://harvardmagazine.com/2000/01/code-is-law-html.

Levine, Yasha 2018. *Surveillance valley: The secret military history of the Internet*: PublicAffairs.

Lewin, Arie Y. 2024. 'Looking ahead for developments that could affect the field of international business', *Journal of International Business Studies*, 56: 557–558.

Li, Shu, Candelon, François & Reeves, Martin 2018. 'Lessons from China's digital battleground', *MIT Sloan Management Review*, 59(4): 1–6.

Lin, Liza. 2024. 'China intensifies push to "delete America" from its technology', *Wall Street Journal*.

Liu, Kevin Ziyu 2024a. 'Making the China data valley–The national integrated big data centre system and local governance', *Journal of Contemporary Asia*, 1–23. www.wsj.com/world/china/china-technology-software-delete-america-2b8ea89f.

Liu, Mingtang & Tsai, Kellee S. 2021. 'Structural power, hegemony, and state capitalism: Limits to China's global economic power', *Politics & Society*, 49(2): 235–267.

Liu, Shaoshan 2024b. 'Escape From Involution: The Overseas Expansion of Chinese Technology Companies'. *The Diplomat*, 9 January.

Liu, Xin 2021. 'Chinese multinational enterprises operating in Western Economies: Huawei in the US and the UK', *Journal of Contemporary China*, 30(129): 368–385.

Liu, Zongyuan Zoe 2024c. 'China Wants To Ditch The Dollar'. *Noema*, 11 January 2024.

Luo, Yadong & Tung, Rosalie L. 2025. 'A multipolar geo-strategy for international business', *Journal of International Business Studies*, 56: 821–829.

Luo, Yadong & Van Assche, Ari 2023. 'The rise of techno-geopolitical uncertainty: Implications of the United States CHIPS and Science Act', *Journal of International Business Studies*, 54: 1423–1440.

Ma, Liang, Christensen, Tom & Zheng, Yueping 2023. 'Government technological capacity and public–private partnerships regarding digital service delivery: Evidence from Chinese cities', *International Review of Administrative Sciences*, 89(1): 95–111.

Mainwaring, Sarah 2020. 'Always in control? Sovereign states in cyberspace', *European Journal of International Security*, 5(2): 215–232.

Majerowicz, Esther & de Carvalho, Miguel Henriques 2024. 'China's expansion into Brazilian digital surveillance markets', *The Information Society*, 40(2): 168–185.

Malkin, Anton 2020. 'The made in China challenge to US structural power: Industrial policy, intellectual property and multinational corporations', *Review of International Political Economy*, 29(2): 538–570.

Martens, Bertin & Zhao, Bo 2021. 'Data access and regime competition: A case study of car data sharing in China', *Big Data & Society*, 8(2): 20539517211046374.

Mau, Steffen 2019. *The Metric Society: On the Quantification of the Social*. John Wiley & Sons.

Mayer, Maximilian & Lu, Yen-Chi 2025. 'Global structures of digital dependence and the rise of technopoles', *New Political Economy*, 1–20. https://doi.org/10.1080/13563467.2025.2497766.

Mazzucato, Mariana 2013. *The Entrepreneurial State*, London: Anthem.

McDowell, Daniel 2019. 'The (Ineffective) Financial statecraft of China's bilateral swap agreements', *Development and Change*, 50(1): 122–143.

McKnight, Scott, Kenney, Martin & Breznitz, Dan 2023. 'Regulating the platform giants: Building and governing China's online economy', *Policy & Internet*, 15(2): 243–265.

McMorrow, Ryan, Olcott, Eleanor, Ruehl, Mercedes & Levingston, Ivan 2024. 'Shein profits double to over $2bn ahead of planned listing'. *Financial Times*, 31 March 2024.

Mezzadra, Sandro & Neilson, Brett 2024. *The Rest and the West: Capital and Power in a Multipolar World*. London: Verso Books.

Mihelj, Sabina 2023. 'Platform nations', *Nations and Nationalism*, 29(1): 10–24.

Mozur, Paul, Kessel, Jonah M. & Chan, Melissa 2019. 'Made in China, Exported to the World: The Surveillance State (Published 2019)'. *New York Times*, 24 April 2019.

Mueller, Milton 2017. *Will the Internet Fragment?: Sovereignty, Globalization and Cyberspace*. Hoboken: John Wiley & Sons.

Mueller, Milton L. & Farhat, Karim 2022. 'Regulation of platform market access by the United States and China: Neo-mercantilism in digital services', *Policy & Internet*, 14(2): 348–367.

Müller, Roland M., Kijl, Björn & Martens, Josef K. J. 2011. 'A comparison of inter-organizational business models of mobile app stores: There is more than open vs. closed', *Journal of Theoretical and Applied Electronic Commerce Research*, 6(2): 63–76.

Munn, Luke 2023. 'Red territory: Forging infrastructural power', *Territory, Politics, Governance*, 11(1): 80–99.

Munn, Luke 2023. 'Red territory: Forging infrastructural power', *Territory, Politics, Governance*, 11(1): 80–99.

Murphree, Michael & Breznitz, Dan 2018. 'Indigenous digital technology standards for development: The case of China', *Journal of International Business Policy*, 1(3): 234–252.

Musacchio, Aldo, Lazzarini, Sergio G. & Aguilera, Ruth V. 2015. 'New varieties of state capitalism: Strategic and governance implications', *Academy of Management Perspectives*, 29(1): 115–131.

Musiani, Francesca, Cogburn, Derrick L., DeNardis, Laura & Levinson, Nanette S. 2016. *The Turn to Infrastructure in Internet Governance*. New York: Palgrave Macmillan.

Nakashima, Ellen 2021. 'NSA surveillance program still raises privacy concerns years after exposure, member of privacy watchdog says'. *Washington Post*, 29 June 2021.

Nanni, Riccardo 2021. 'The 'China'question in mobile internet standard-making: Insights from expert interviews', *Telecommunications Policy*, 45(6): 102151.

Narayan, Devika 2022. 'Platform capitalism and cloud infrastructure: Theorizing a hyper-scalable computing regime', *Environment and Planning A: Economy and Space*, 54(5): 911–929.

National Security Agency 2022. 'Cybersecurity Collaboration Center' [Online]. www.nsa.gov/About/Cybersecurity-Collaboration-Center/.

Naughton, Barry 2020a. 'Chinese industrial policy and the digital silk road: The case of Alibaba in Malaysia', *Asia Policy*, 27(1): 23–39.

Naughton, Barry 2020b. *The Rise of China's Industrial Policy, 1978 to 2020*. Mexico City: National Autonomous University of Mexico.

Naughton, Barry 2021. 'What's Behind China's Regulatory Storm'. *Wall Street Journal*, 12 December.

Naughton, Barry & Tsai, Kellee S. 2015. *State Capitalism, Institutional Adaptation, and the Chinese Miracle*. Cambridge: Cambridge University Press.

Neaher, Giulia, Bray, David A., Mueller-Kaler, Julian & Schatz, Benjamin 2021. *Standardizing the Future: How Can the United States Navigate the Geopolitics of International Technology Standards?* [Online]. www.jstor.org/stable/resrep36741.

Newlove-Eriksson, Lindy 2022. *Critical Infrastructure at the Dawn of a Techno-Organizational Shift: Accountability and Public-Private Governance*. PhD, KTH Royal Institute of Technology.

Nikou Asgari, Alan Smith, Wilson, Kevin & Douglas, Ray 2024. 'In charts: Why European stock markets are in crisis'. *Financial Times*, 3 March 2024.

Nitzberg, Mark & Zysman, John 2022. 'Algorithms, data, and platforms: the diverse challenges of governing AI', *Journal of European Public Policy*, 29(11): 1753–1778.

Nölke, Andreas 2022. 'Geoeconomic infrastructures: Building Chinese-Russian alternatives to SWIFT', In Braun, Benjamin & Koddenbrock, Kai (eds.) *Capital Claims: The Political Economy of Global Finance*, pp. 147–166. London: Routledge.

Nowak, Jörg, Rolf, Steven & Wei, Wei 2022. 'Leapfrog Logistics: Digital platforms, infrastructure, and labor in Brazil and China' [Online]. Jain Family Institute. www.phenomenalworld.org/analysis/leapfrog-logistics/.

O'Dwyer, Rachel 2023. *Tokens: The Future of Money in the Age of the Platform*. London: Verso Books.

O'Grady, Vaughan 2024. 'Alibaba plans Vietnam data centre to meet localisation requirements'. *Developing Telecoms*, 2 May 2024.

O'Mara, Margaret 2020. *The Code: Silicon Valley and the Remaking of America*. New York: Penguin Books.

Oh, Yoon Ah & No, Suyeon 2020. 'The patterns of state-firm coordination in China's private sector internationalization: China's mergers and acquisitions in Southeast Asia', *The Pacific Review*, 33(6): 873–899.

Oyedemi, Toks Dele 2021. 'Digital coloniality and "Next Billion Users": the political economy of Google Station in Nigeria', *Information, Communication & Society*, 24(3): 329–343.

Pape, Fabian 2022. 'Governing global liquidity: Federal reserve swap lines and the international dimension of US monetary policy', *New Political Economy*, 27(3): 455–472.

Payne, Sebastian & Fildes, Nic 2020. 'UK to Ban Installation of Huawei 5 G Equipment from September'. *Financial Times*, 30 November 2020.

Pearson, Margaret, Rithmire, Meg & Tsai, Kellee S. 2021. 'Party-state capitalism in China', *Current History*, 120(827): 207–213.

Peck, Jamie & Phillips, Rachel 2021. 'The platform conjuncture', *Sociologica*, 14(3): 73–99.

Peck, Jamie & Tickell, Adam 1994. 'Searching for a new institutional fix: The After-Fordist crisis and the global-local disorder', In Amin, Ash (ed.) *Post-Fordism*, pp. 280–315. Cambridge: Blackwell.

Pettis, Michael 2011. 'An exorbitant burden: Why keeping the dollar as the world's reserve currency is a massive drag on the struggling US economy', *Foreign Policy*, 7. https://foreignpolicy.com/2011/09/07/an-exorbitant-burden.

Pitron, Guillaume 2023. *The Dark Cloud: How the Digital World is Costing the Earth*. London: Scribe Publications.

Plantin, Jean-Christophe 2021. 'The geopolitical hijacking of open networking: The case of Open RAN', *European Journal of Communication*, 36(4): 404–417.

Plantin, Jean-Christophe & De Seta, Gabriele 2019. 'WeChat as infrastructure: The techno-nationalist shaping of Chinese digital platforms', *Chinese Journal of Communication*, 12(3): 257–273.

Plantin, Jean-Christophe, Lagoze, Carl, Edwards, Paul N & Sandvig, Christian 2018. 'Infrastructure studies meet platform studies in the age of Google and Facebook', *New Media & Society*, 20(1): 293–310.

Pomfret, James, Yao, Kevin & Zhang, Ellen 2024. 'China's Xi Jinping Summons "New Productive Forces," But Old Questions Linger'. *Reuters*, 5 March 2024.

Powers, Shawn M. & Jablonski, Michael 2015. *The Real Cyber War: The Political Economy of Internet Freedom*. Urbana: University of Illinois Press.

Priyandita, Gatra, van der Kley, Dirk & Herscovitch, Benjamin 2022. 'Localization and China's Tech Success in Indonesia' [Online]. https://carnegieendowment.org/files/van_der_Kley_et_al_China_Indonesia_final_1.pdf.

Rahman, K. Sabeel 2018. 'Regulating informational infrastructure: Internet platforms as the new public utilities', *Georgetown Law and Technology Review*, 22: 234–251.

Rakhmat, Zulfikar 2022. 'China's Digital Silk Road in Indonesia Progress and Implications' [Online]. www.jstor.org/stable/resrep45243.

Ravenhill, John 2017. 'The political economy of the Trans-Pacific Partnership: A '21st Century' trade agreement?', *New Political Economy*, 22(5): 573–594.

Ren, Daniel. 2022. 'BYD to use Baidu's autonomous driving technology as it takes on Tesla'. *South China Morning Post*, 1 March 2022.

Rikap, Cecilia 2024. 'Varieties of corporate innovation systems and their interplay with global and national systems: Amazon, Facebook, Google and Microsoft's strategies to produce and appropriate artificial intelligence', *Review of International Political Economy*, 31(6): 1735–1763.

Rikap, Cecilia & Lundvall, Bengt-Åke 2021. *Digital Innovation Race*. Cham: Springer.

Robert, Greene & Paul, Triolo. 2020. 'Will China Control the Global Internet Via its Digital Silk Road?' [Online]. Carnegie Endowment for International Peace. https://policycommons.net/artifacts/434249/will-china-control-the-global-internet-via-its-digital-silk-road/.

Roberts, Huw, Cowls, Josh, Morley, Jessica et al. 2021. 'The Chinese approach to artificial intelligence: An analysis of policy, ethics, and regulation', *AI & SOCIETY*, 36(1): 59–77.

References

Robinson, William I. 2020. *The Global Police State*. London: Pluto Press.

Rodon Modol, Joan & Eaton, Ben 2021. 'Digital infrastructure evolution as generative entrenchment: The formation of a core–periphery structure', *Journal of Information Technology*, 36(4): 342–364.

Rolf, Steve & Schindler, Seth 2023. 'The US–China rivalry and the emergence of state platform capitalism', *Environment and Planning A: Economy and Space*, 55(5): 1255–1280, Online First.

Rolf, Steven 2021. *China's Uneven and Combined Development*. Cham: Springer.

Rosen, Daniel & Gloudeman, Lauren. 2021. *Understanding US-China Decoupling: Macro Trends and Industry Impacts* [Online]. https://rhg.com/research/us-china-decoupling/.

Rühlig, Tim 2023. 'Chinese influence through technical standardization power', *Journal of Contemporary China*, 32(139): 54–72.

Ruiz, Javier & Savona, Maria 2023. The US Turn is Reshaping the Geopolitics of Digital Trade: What Does This Mean for the UK? *Centre for Inclusive Trade Policy* [Online]. https://citp.ac.uk/publications/the-us-turn-is-reshaping-the-geopolitics-of-digital-trade-what-does-this-mean-for-the-uk [Accessed 5 December.

Ryan, Maria & Burman, Stephen 2024. 'The United States–China "tech war": Decoupling and the case of Huawei', *Global Policy*, 15(2): 355–367.

Ryugen, Hideaki & Hiroyuki, Akiyama 2020. 'China leads the way on global standards for 5 G and beyond'. *Financial Times*, 4 August 2020.

Sadowski, Jathan 2020. 'The internet of landlords: Digital platforms and new mechanisms of rentier capitalism', *Antipode*, 52(2): 562–580.

Salgado, Richard 2023. *Undersea Cables, Hyperscalers, and National Security*. Stanford: Hoover Institution.

Saraiva, Augusta 2024. 'US Pushes for Global AI Regulations at UN'. *Bloomberg*, 2024-03-14T18:01:27.058Z.

Sassen, Saskia 1996. *Losing Control? Sovereignty in the Age of Globalization*. New York: Columbia University Press.

Sastry, Girish, Heim, Lennart, Belfield, Haydn et al. 2024. 'Computing power and the governance of artificial intelligence', *arXiv preprint arXiv:2402.08797*.

Schindler, Seth, Alami, Ilias, DiCarlo, Jessica et al. 2023. 'The second cold war: US-China competition for centrality in infrastructure, digital, production, and finance networks', *Geopolitics*, 29(4): 1083–1120.

Schindler, Seth, Alami, Ilias, DiCarlo, Jessica et al. 2024. 'The second cold war: US-China competition for centrality in infrastructure, digital, production, and finance networks', *Geopolitics*, 29(4): 1083–1120.

Schindler, Seth & and Rolf, Steve 2024. 'Geostrategic globalization: US–China rivalry, corporate strategy, and the new global economy', *Globalizations*, 22(6): 897–914.

Schindler, Seth & Kanai, J. Miguel 2021. 'Getting the territory right: Infrastructure-led development and the re-emergence of spatial planning strategies', *Regional Studies*, 55(1): 40–51.

Schindler, Seth & Marvin, Simon 2018. 'Constructing a universal logic of urban control? International standards for city data, management, and interoperability', *City*, 22(2): 298–307.

Schmidt, Eric 2022. 'Address to the SCSP Global Emerging Technology Summit: Eric Schmidt, 23 September' [Online]. www.youtube.com/watch?v=aE3kz3zzA0Y&t=101s.

Schwartz, Herman Mark 2017. 'Much Ventured, Much Gained: The US Innovation State', *International Studies Review*, 19(2): 326–328.

Schwartz, Herman Mark 2019. 'American hegemony: intellectual property rights, dollar centrality, and infrastructural power', *Review of International Political Economy*, 26(3): 490–519.

Seaman, John 2020. 'China and the new geopolitics of technical standardization', *French Institute of International Relations*. www.ifri.org/en/publications/notes-de-lifri/china-and-new-geopolitics-technical-standardization, accessed on, 25(03): 2020.

Segal, Adam 2018. 'When China rules the web: Technology in service of the state', *Foreign Affairs*, 97, 10.

Shambaugh, David 2020. 'China's long march to global power', In Shambaugh, David (ed.) *China and the World*, pp. 343–367. Oxford: Oxford University Press.

Sheehan, Matt 2024. *Tracing the Roots of China's AI Regulations* [Online]. https://carnegieendowment.org/research/2024/02/tracing-the-roots-of-chinas-ai-regulations?lang=en.

Shelton, Taylor, Zook, Matthew & Wiig, Alan 2015. 'The "actually existing smart city"', *Cambridge Journal of Regions, Economy and Society*, 8(1): 13–25.

Shen, Hong 2018. 'Building a Digital Silk Road? Situating the Internet in China's Belt and Road Initiative', *International Journal of Communication*, 12: 2683–2701.

Shen, Hong 2020. 'China's Tech Giants: Baidu, Alibaba, Tencent' [Online]. www.kas.de/documents/288143/4843367/panorama_digital_asia_v3b_HongShen.pdf/a21ab7b9-8e37-acfa-19a3-955a5881088f.

Shen, Hong 2022a. *Alibaba: Infrastructuring Global China*. London: Routledge.

Shen, Hong 2022b. 'How to understand China's globalized digital infrastructure', *Centre for International Governance Innovation*. www.cigionline.org/articles/how-to-understand-chinas-globalized-digital-infrastructure.

Shen, Hong & He, Yujia 2022. 'The geopolitics of infrastructuralized platforms: The case of Alibaba', In Jack Linchuan Qiu, Peter K. Yu, Elisa Oreglia (eds.) *The Geopolitics of Chinese Internets*, pp. 29-46. London: Routledge.

Shepardson, David 2024. 'US says leading AI companies join safety consortium to address risks'. *Reuters*, 8 February 2024.

Simonite, Tom 2021. '3 Years After the Maven Uproar, Google Cozies to the Pentagon'. *Wired*, 18 November.

Sohn, Tim 2015. 'Trevor Paglen Plumbs the Internet'. *New Yorker*, 22 September 2015.

Sontag, Sherry, Drew, Christopher & Drew, Annette Lawrence 1998. *Blind Man's Bluff: The Untold Story of American Submarine Espionage*. New York: Public Affairs.

Sperber, Nathan 2019. 'The many lives of state capitalism: From classical Marxism to free-market advocacy', *History of the Human Sciences*, 32(3): 100–124.

Srnicek, Nick 2017. *Platform Capitalism*. John Wiley & Sons.

Staab, Philipp 2024. *Markets and Power in Digital Capitalism*. Manchester: Manchester University Press.

Starrs, Sean Kenji & Germann, Julian 2021. 'Responding to the China challenge in techno-nationalism: Divergence between Germany and the United States', *Development and Change*, 52(5): 1122–1146.

Steil, Ben, Della Rocca, Benjamin & Walker, Dinah 2024. 'Central bank currency swaps tracker' [Online]. Council on Foreign Relations.

Sullivan, Jake 2022. 'Remarks by National Security Advisor Jake Sullivan on the Biden-Harris Administration's National Security Strategy' [Online]. Washington, DC: The White House. www.whitehouse.gov/briefing-room/speeches-remarks/2022/10/13/remarks-by-national-security-advisor-jake-sullivan-on-the-biden-harris-administrations-national-security-strategy/.

Takeda, Kentaro & Ban, Masaharu 2024. 'More subsea cables bypass China as Sino-U.S. tensions grow'. *Nikkei Asia*, 11 May 2024.

Tang, Frank & Nulimaimaiti, Mia 2023. 'China's tech giants off leash after crackdown, and Beijing is counting on them'. *South China Morning Post*, 12 july 2023.

Tang, Min 2020. 'Huawei versus the United States? The geopolitics of exterritorial Internet infrastructure', *International Journal of Communication*, 14, 22.

Tarnoff, Ben 2022. *Internet for the People: The Fight for Our Digital Future*. Verso Books.

Tassinari, Mattia 2018. *Capitalising Economic Power in the US: Industrial Strategy in the Neoliberal Era*. Cham: Springer.

TechNode 2023. 'Tencent Cloud Unveils Latest AI Solutions in Malaysia' [Online]. https://technode.global/2023/12/22/tencent-cloud-unveils-latest-ai-solutions-in-malaysia/.
The White House 2018. 'National Cyber Strategy of the United States of America' [Online]. Washington, DC. https://trumpwhitehouse.archives.gov/wp-content/uploads/2018/09/National-Cyber-Strategy.pdf.
The White House 2022a. 'FACT SHEET: CHIPS and Science Act Will Lower Costs, Create Jobs, Strengthen Supply Chains, and Counter China' [Online]. www.whitehouse.gov/briefing-room/statements-releases/2022/08/09/fact-sheet-chips-and-science-act-will-lower-costs-create-jobs-strengthen-supply-chains-and-counter-china/.
The White House 2022b. 'Indo-Pacific Strategy of the United States' [Online]. www.whitehouse.gov/wp-content/uploads/2022/02/U.S.-Indo-Pacific-Strategy.pdf.
The White House 2023. 'United States Government National Standards Strategy for Critical and Emerging Technology' [Online]. Washington, DC. www.whitehouse.gov/wp-content/uploads/2023/05/US-Gov-National-Standards-Strategy-2023.pdf.
Thomas, Llewellyn D. W., Ritala, Paavo, Karhu, Kimmo & Heiskala, Mikko 2024. 'Vertical and horizontal complementarities in platform ecosystems', *Innovation*, 27(3): 369–393.
Thun, Eric & Sturgeon, Timothy 2019. 'When global technology meets local standards: Reassessing China's communications policy in the age of platform innovation', In Brandt, Loren & Rawski, Thomas G. (eds.) *Policy, Regulation and Innovation in China's Electricity and Telecom Industries*, pp. 177–220. Cambridge: Cambridge University Press.
To, Yvette 2023. 'Friends and foes: Rethinking the party and Chinese big tech', *New Political Economy*, 28(2): 299–314.
Törnberg, Petter 2023. 'Platforms as States: The Rise of Governance through Data Power', *Data Power in Action*. Bristol University Press.
Townsend, Anthony M. 2013. *Smart cities: Big data, civic hackers, and the quest for a new utopia*. New York: WW Norton.
Triolo, Paul 2022. 'The Digital Silk Road and the evolving role of Chinese technology companies', In Nouwens, David Gordon; Meia (ed.) *The Digital Silk Road*, pp. 79–81. London: Routledge.
Tse, Edward 2015. *China's Disruptors: How Alibaba, Xiaomi, Tencent, and Other Companies are Changing the Rules of Business*. New York: Penguin.
Tugendhat, Tom 2021. 'China's Communist Party Behind Surveillance Capitalism'. *Daily Mail*, 28 August 2021.

Turner, Oliver & Parmar, Inderjeet 2020. *The United States in the Indo-Pacific: Obama's Legacy and the Trump Transition*. Manchester: Manchester University Press.

Tusikov, Natasha 2021. 'Internet platforms weaponizing choke points', In Drezner, Daniel W., Farrell, Henry & Newman, Abraham L. (eds.) *The Uses and Abuses of Weaponized Interdependence*, pp. 133–148. Washington, DC: Brookings Institution Press.

U.S. Department of Defense 2018. *Assessment on U.S. Defense Implications of China's Expanding Global Access* [Online]. Washington, DC.

U.S. State Department 2021. 'The Clean Network' [Online]. https://2017-2021.state.gov/the-clean-network/.

USCC Staff 2022. *LOGINK: Risks from China's Promotion of a Global Logistics Management Platform* [Online]. www.uscc.gov/sites/default/files/2022-09/LOGINK-Risks_from_Chinas_Promotion_of_a_Global_Logistics_Management_Platform.pdf.

van Apeldoorn, Bastiaan & de Graaff, Naná 2022. 'The state in global capitalism before and after the COVID-19 crisis', *Contemporary Politics*, 28(3): 1–22.

van Apeldoorn, Bastiaan, Veselinovič, Jaša & de Graaff, Naná 2023. *Trump and the Remaking of American Grand Strategy: The Shift from Open Door Globalism to Economic Nationalism*. Cham: Springer.

van der Vlist, Fernando, Helmond, Anne & Ferrari, Fabian 2024. 'Big AI: Cloud infrastructure dependence and the industrialisation of artificial intelligence', *Big Data & Society*, 11(1): 20539517241232630.

Van Dijck, José 2020. 'Governing digital societies: Private platforms, public values', *Computer Law & Security Review*, 36: 36105377.

van Dijck, José & Lin, Jian 2022. 'Deplatformization, platform governance and global geopolitics: Interview with José van Dijck', *Communication and the Public*, 7(2): 59–66.

Varoufakis, Yanis 2024. *Technofeudalism: What Killed Capitalism*. Hoboken: Melville House.

Vishnoi, Abhishek & Yang, Charlotte. 2024. 'China's $6.3 Trillion Stock Selloff Is Getting Uglier by the Day'. *Bloomberg*, 19 January 2024.

Wade, Robert H. 2017. 'The American paradox: ideology of free markets and the hidden practice of directional thrust', *Cambridge Journal of Economics*, 41(3): 859–880.

Walker, Richard A. 2006. 'The boom and the bombshell: The new economy bubble and the San Francisco Bay area', In *The Changing Economic Geography of Globalization*, pp. 121–147. London: Routledge.

Wang, Hongying & Yu, Hanzhi 2022. 'Aspiring rule-makers: Chinese business actors in global governance', *Journal of Chinese Governance*, 7(1): 137–157.

Wei, Yifan, Ang, Yuen Yuen & Jia, Nan 2023. 'The promise and pitfalls of government guidance funds in China', *The China Quarterly*, 256: 939–959.

Weichert, Brandon 2024. 'USS Jimmy Carter is an Incredible and Top Secret Seawolf-Class Submarine | The National Interest'. *The National Interest*, 2024-04-09T15:17-04:00.

Weiss, Linda 2014. *America Inc.?: Innovation and Enterprise in the National Security State*. Ithaca: Cornell University Press.

Weiss, Linda 2021. 'Re-emergence of great power conflict and US economic statecraft', *World Trade Review*, 20(2): 152–168.

Weiss, Linda & Thurbon, Elizabeth 2020. 'Developmental state or economic statecraft? Where, why and how the difference matters', *New Political Economy*, 126(3): 472–489.

Westermeier, Carola 2020. 'Money is data – the platformization of financial transactions', *Information, Communication & Society*, 23(14): 2047–2063.

White, Edward & Yu, Sun 2023. 'Xi Jinping's dream of a Chinese military-industrial complex'. *Financial Times*, 19 June 2023.

Whittaker, D. Hugh, Sturgeon, Timothy, Okita, Toshie & Zhu, Tianbiao 2020. *Compressed Development: Time and Timing in Economic and Social Development*. Oxford: Oxford University Press.

Wijaya, Trissia & Jayasuriya, Kanishka 2024. 'A new multipolar order: Combined development, state forms and new business classes', *International Affairs*, 100(5): 2133–2152.

Wikimedia 2013. 'File:Upstream slide of the PRISM presentation.jpg – Wikimedia Commons' [Online]. https://commons.wikimedia.org/wiki/File:Upstream_slide_of_the_PRISM_presentation.jpg.

Wu, Yi 2022. 'The China Standards 2035 Strategy: Analyzing Recent Developments'. *China Briefing*, 26 July 2022.

Xinhua 2025. 'Xi urges promoting healthy and orderly development of AI'. *Xinhua*, April 29.

Yates, JoAnne & Murphy, Craig N. 2022. 'Introduction: Standards and the global economy', *Business History Review*, 96(1): 3–15.

Yoo, Christopher S. & Mueller, Alexander 2024. 'Crouching tiger, hidden agenda?: The emergence of China in the global internet standard-setting arena', *Federal Communications Law Journal*, 145–216.

Yue, Aobo, Mao, Chao, Wang, Zhuoqi, Peng, Wuxue & Zhao, Shuming 2024. 'Finding the pioneers of China's smart cities: From the perspective of construction efficiency and construction performance', *Technological Forecasting and Social Change*, 204: 123410.

Zeng, Jing & Glaister, Keith W. 2016. 'Competitive dynamics between multinational enterprises and local internet platform companies in the virtual market in China', *British Journal of Management*, 27(3): 479–496.

Zhang, Lin 2025. 'Market in the Fragmented State: Alibaba and the Chinese Governance Regime of Big Tech', *Social Media + Society*, 11(2): 20563051251340147.

Zhang, Lin & Lan, Tu 2023. 'The new whole state system: Reinventing the Chinese state to promote innovation', *Environment and Planning A: Economy and Space*, 55(1): 201–221.

Zheng, Sarah 2024. 'Alibaba Discloses State Ownership in More Than 12 Business Units'. *Bloomberg*, 26 February 2024.

Acknowledgement

This work was supported by the UKRI Economic and Social Research Council [grant number ES/S012532/1] as part of the ESRC Centre for Digital Futures at Work.

Cambridge Elements

Reinventing Capitalism

Arie Y. Lewin
Duke University

Arie Y. Lewin is Professor Emeritus of Strategy and International Business at Duke University, Fuqua School of Business. He is an Elected Fellow of the Academy of International Business and a Recipient of the Academy of Management inaugural Joanne Martin Trailblazer Award. Previously, he was Editor-in-Chief of *Management and Organization Review* (2015–2021) and the *Journal of International Business Studies* (2000–2007), founding Editor-in-Chief of Organization Science (1989–2007), and Convener of Organization Science Winter Conference (1990–2012). His research centers on studies of organizations' adaptation as co-evolutionary systems, the emergence of new organizational forms, and adaptive capabilities of innovating and imitating organizations. His current research focuses on de-globalization and decoupling, the Fourth Industrial Revolution, and the renewal of capitalism.

Till Talaulicar
University of Erfurt

Till Talaulicar holds the Chair of Organization and Management at the University of Erfurt where he is also the Dean of the Faculty of Economics, Law and Social Sciences. His main research expertise is in the areas of corporate governance and the responsibilities of the corporate sector in modern societies. Professor Talaulicar is Editor-in-Chief of *Corporate Governance: An International Review*, Senior Editor of Management and Organization Review and serves on the Editorial Board of Organization Science. Moreover, he has been Founding Member and Chairperson of the Board of the International Corporate Governance Society (2014–2020).

Editorial Advisory Board

Paul S. Adler, *University of Southern California, USA*
Ruth V. Aguilera, *Northeastern University, USA*
Christina Ahmadjian, *Hitotsubashi University, Japan*
Helena Barnard, *University of Pretoria, South Africa*
Jay Barney, *University of Utah, USA*
Jerry Davis, *University of Michigan, USA*
Steve Denning, *Forbes*
Rebecca Henderson, *Harvard University, USA*
Thomas Hutzschenreuter, *TU München, Germany*
Tarun Khanna, *Harvard University, USA*
Peter G. Klein, *Baylor University, USA*
Costas Markides, *London Business School, UK*
Anita McGahan, *University of Toronto, Canada*
Rita McGrath, *Columbia University, USA*
Heather McGregor, *Edinburgh Business School, UK*
Alan Meyer, *University of Oregon, USA*
Katrin Muff, *LUISS University Rome, Italy*
Peter Murmann, *University of St. Gallen, Switzerland*

Tsuyoshi Numagami, *Hitotsubashi University, Japan*
Margit Osterloh, *University of Basel, Switzerland*
Andreas Georg Scherer, *University of Zurich, Switzerland*
Blair Sheppard, *PwC, USA*
Jeffrey Sonnenfeld, *Yale University, USA*
John Sutton, *LSE, UK*
David Teece, *UC Berkeley, USA*
Anne S. Tsui, *University of Notre Dame, USA*
Alain Verbeke, *University of Calgary, Canada*
Henk Volberda, *University of Amsterdam, The Netherlands*
Mira Wilkins, *Florida International University, USA*
Sarah Williamson, *FCLTGlobal, USA*
Arjen van Witteloostuijn, *VU Amsterdam, The Netherlands*
George Yip, *Imperial College London, UK*

About the Series

This series seeks to feature explorations about the crisis of legitimacy facing capitalism today, including the increasing income and wealth gap, the decline of the middle class, threats to employment due to globalization and digitalization, undermined trust in institutions, discrimination against minorities, global poverty and pollution. Being grounded in a business and management perspective, the series incorporates contributions from multiple disciplines on the causes of the current crisis and potential solutions to renew capitalism.

Panmure House is the final and only remaining home of Adam Smith, Scottish philosopher and 'Father of modern economics.' Smith occupied the House between 1778 and 1790, during which time he completed the final editions of his master works: The Theory of Moral Sentiments and The Wealth of Nations. Other great luminaries and thinkers of the Scottish Enlightenment visited Smith regularly at the House across this period. Their mission is to provide a world-class twenty-first-century centre for social and economic debate and research, convening in the name of Adam Smith to effect positive change and forge global, future-focussed networks.

Cambridge Elements

Reinventing Capitalism

Elements in the Series

From Financialisation to Innovation in UK Big Pharma: AstraZeneca and GlaxoSmithKline
Öner Tulum, Antonio Andreoni, William Lazonick

Comparing Capitalisms for an Unknown Future: Societal Processes and Transformative Capacity
Gordon Redding

The Future of Work in Diverse Economic Systems: The Varieties of Capitalism Perspective
Daniel Friel

Transforming our Critical Systems: How Can We Achieve the Systemic Change the World Needs?
Gerardus van der Zanden and Rozanne Henzen

Aberrant Capitalism: The Decay and Revival of Customer Capitalism
Hunter Hastings and Stephen Denning

Private Equity and the Demise of the Local: The Loss of Community Economic Power and Autonomy
Maryann Feldman and Martin Kenney

The Transformation of Boeing from Technological Leadership to Financial Engineering and Decline
Charles McMillan

The Fading Light of Democratic Capitalism: How Pervasive Cronyism and Restricted Suffrage Are Destroying Democratic Capitalism as a National Ideal . . . And What To Do About It
Malcolm S. Salter

State-Owned Enterprises as Institutional Actors in Contemporary Capitalism and Beyond
Olivier Butzbach, Douglas B. Fuller, Gerhard Schnyder and Luda Svystunova

Towards More Inclusive Varieties of Capitalism
Simon Collinson

The Post-Managerial Era of Capitalism
Hunter Hastings

State Platform Capitalism: The United States, China, and the Global Battle for Digital Supremacy
Steve Rolf and Seth Schindler

A full series listing is available at: www.cambridge.org/RECA

For EU product safety concerns, contact us at Calle de José Abascal, 56–1°, 28003 Madrid, Spain or eugpsr@cambridge.org.

www.ingramcontent.com/pod-product-compliance
Lightning Source LLC
LaVergne TN
LVHW011849060526
838200LV00054B/4254